Feeling Strong, Feeling Free: Movement Exploration for Young Children

Feeling Strong, Feeling Free: Movement Exploration for Young Children

by
Molly Sullivan

A 1982−83 *Comprehensive* Membership Benefit

National Association for the Education of Young
Children
Washington, D.C.

Book Design: Melanie Rose White
Photo credits:
Cathy Nelson p. 152
Molly Sullivan p. 25
Susan Dinkelspiel Stern pp. 12, 15, 42, 51, 58, 64, 74, 79, 82, 96, 153

Second Printing, February 1985.

Library of Congress Catalog Card Number: 82-61730
ISBN Catalog Number: #0-912674-82-2
NAEYC #100

National Association for the Education of Young Children
1834 Connecticut Avenue, N.W.
Washington, DC 20009

Printed in the United States of America.

To Mary Wilson Sullivan

Contents

Acknowledgments

Lynn Steinman who critiqued this book with the enormous thought and energy she gives to all she touches.

Veronica Sherborne, Ruth Zaporah, Terry Sendgraff, Al Wunder, and Byron Brown, all great movement/dance teachers. In this book, I pass on many of their teachings.

Hildred Yost for her enlightening comments over the years.

The teachers, parents, and children who have worked with me, encouraged me, and from whom I have learned so much. The list is very long, but most recently Martin Luther King Children's Center of Berkeley who allowed me to work with and photograph their children, and in particular Kay Dols for her great interest and perceptive comments.

Barbara Priest for her thoughtful preparation of this manuscript.

Gabrielle Nicholson and Isaac Nicholson who taught me most clearly what children need.

Frank Mark for the priceless gifts of time and support.

Introduction

The joy of moving brings pleasure to children and adults. Adults, in recent years, are rediscovering the joy of movement as they jog, dance, bicycle, or take up tennis. The impetus for these activities comes in the form of concern for physical and mental health.

Unfortunately, the joy of moving is not an integral part of movement education in all programs for young children. Children need opportunities to use movement as a vehicle for creative expression, and to develop confidence in their ability to move. Some programs, through excess structuring, limit a child's scope for experimentation. Many early childhood educators and physical development specialists voice concern that often programs in physical education stress isolated attention to the body and ignore the related emotional, social, cognitive, and creative development of the child.

Movement exploration is a method of teaching that considers the development of the total child. In contrast to programmed activities for physical development, movement exploration activities encourage the child to apply problem-solving techniques and to explore fantasies and relationships with others. With movement exploration activities children can find, as well, a wide range of body experiences through which they will naturally develop motor skills and knowledge of the operation of their own bodies. A child's self-concept can grow in positive directions because the movement exploration teacher, by establishing a nonjudgmental technique, demonstrates respect for each child's abilities.

This book grows out of a belief in the need for movement exploration programs that fulfill the objectives above. Applying the objectives can be difficult, but techniques provided in this book will be useful to teachers who share this belief and who would like to structure appropriate movement activities for groups of children.

The book is divided into four parts. The first part suggests various options for incorporating movement activities into the school day and provides information which will be useful to the teacher in planning movement exploration sessions. The second part is for those who work with three- and four-year-olds. The third part is for teachers of five-, six-, seven-, and eight-year-olds. Within Parts II and III are information and activities for those age groups. The fourth part consists of activities for one child and one adult working together. This special group of activities is not appropriate for use in planning a group movement session but may be of great use during less formal times with children. It is suggested that the reader skim the portions that do not pertain directly to her or his particular children's age group. Ideally, the entire book should be read so that the reader has a deeper understanding of the concepts and goals for children.

This book is meant to be useful. It is intended to furnish techniques and a format for teaching movement exploration that will work—that will make the experience fulfilling and joyful for both teachers and children.

Part I: The Framework

Chapter 1: Preparing to teach movement

Elements of movement

The elements of movement upon which all the activities in this book are based were defined by Rudolf Laban in 1948 in a book called *Modern Educational Dance*. They have since become a standard approach for many dance and movement teachers. As you work with these elements, they will become so familiar that you will instinctively refer to them when it is appropriate to extend a movement activity. The elements and definitions are modified here so that they may be referred to easily as you read the book.

Body awareness: The shape of the body in space, where the different body parts are, how the body moves and rests, the body's behavior when combined with other bodies, how the voice is a part of the body.

Force and time: Being limp, being energetic, being light, being fluid, being staccato, being slow, being quick.

Space: Where the body is in a room, the level (high—erect posture or in the air; middle—examples are crawling or stooped; low—on the floor), direction (forward, backward, sideways), size (bigness, smallness), path through space, extensions of body parts into space.

Locomotion: Movement through space at various levels (lowest—wriggling, rolling, scooting; middle—crawling, crouching, using four limbs (ape walk); highest—walking, running, skipping, galloping, sliding, leaping, hopping, jumping).

Weight: Relationship of body to ground, ways to manage body weight in motion and in relationship to others, collapses, understanding momentum.

Working with others: Combining with others to solve problems, to develop trust, to explore strength and sensitivity, to feel a sense of union with others.

Isolations: How various individual body parts (head, shoulders, arms, hands, elbows, wrists, neck, back, upper torso, ribs, hips, legs, knees, ankles, feet) can move (swinging, jerking, twisting, shaking, lifting, tensing, relaxing, becoming fluid, pressing, gliding, floating, flicking, slashing, punching, dabbing).

Repetitions: Getting to know a movement and how it feels when repeated often; being able to repeat a shape or action.

Logistics

Ways to incorporate activities during the day

The movement activities in this book can be used in a classroom in a variety of ways. The entire group can work together on a regular basis doing a number of different activities for a period of time, usually ranging from 15 minutes to 1 hour. Traditionally, a movement specialist works with a class in this manner. When the entire group participates, there is no need to provide an alternate activity. More important, the teacher can deal with the dynamics of the whole class to develop group interaction.

As an alternative, a portion of the class can work together on a regular basis doing a number of different activities for a specified period of time. An appropriate group of children would number between 8 and 15 with one adult for every 5 three- and four-year-olds. With older children, one adult is appropriate for every 10 to 15 children. Groups of this size are large enough to generate energy between members but small enough to allow the teacher to recognize how each individual deals with the materials. The teacher can achieve a sense of intimacy and successfully manage a group this size while assistants, parents, or volunteers take the children not participating in movement activities to the library, outside to play a game, or to do an art project.

The group can participate in movement sessions daily in the classroom, such as relaxation following lunch. With this practice the teacher is able to create in-depth knowledge of a specific activity for children. Also, the activity can become an expected ritual, which is a centering experience for children. Or, while leading one movement session daily at a designated time, the teacher can select a *different* activity each day, thereby providing a surprise element for the students.

One approach that integrates movement activities into the total program is leading activities in a random fashion in the classroom, on the playground, or in a park. With this method the teacher does not need to provide a separate time slot with transitions before and after the activity.

An adult could work with individual children for a period of time in the classroom or in the park (see Part IV). With this approach the adult and child can develop a closer relationship and the adult can attend to the child's particular strengths and weaknesses.

Selecting a space

Ideally you should lead movement sessions in a space separate from the classroom. A movement activities area requires these elements:

- a resilient wood floor to prevent injury
- adequate ventilation and heating
- few distractions
- uncluttered open space to prevent collisions with furniture and other objects
- private space to prevent inhibition and to enhance quality of movement

If the ideal space is not available, options must be examined. Some ideas for making space more appropriate are discussed in the sections which follow.

Location. The classroom has the advantage of familiarity and the ease of accessibility. In most centers and schools space is limited and distractions numerous. You and/or the children can push furniture against one wall, or divide the group in half in order to have more space and more control.

In an open classroom arrangement, you can use the meeting space with three- and four-year-olds. That is usually the best arrangement for this age group. A small group of children can do a movement session while a larger group works on other activities in the classroom.

Taking the children to a space other than a classroom holds the advantage of setting a mood for a special set of experiences. Children can associate movement activities with this space and, they can move more innovatively and with more concentration. The teacher may locate a dance studio or a gymnasium within walking distance if there is not an appropriate space on the school site.

Doing movement activities outdoors can be difficult unless the activities are closely focused. Weather may be a problem much of the year, distractions are great, and boundaries are usually difficult to define. However, activities held on the grass have a wonderful informality. After exposure to some of the activities in this guide, children often spontaneously experiment with the material on playgrounds or on trips to the park.

Size. You must define movement activities or children will wander off. This can happen in an interior space that is too large. Marking boundaries with tape or objects enables children to feel the group around them and the teacher's connection with the group. Children inevitably collide in a too-small space, distracting everyone. A small space can be used only if the activities are designed to work in an area that size, such as with "Clap, Clap, Clap Your Hands," or if the size of the group is reduced.

Floor surface. A movement activities teacher should use a wooden floor with spring to it (not one placed on concrete) for best results with the class and for maximum prevention of harm to children's bodies. Such a floor is good to land on, slide on, and lie on. A carpeted floor can be inviting to lie on and has a softness nice for falling onto. However, rug burns can occur if a child slides across carpet. In modern school construction, many floors are laid over concrete and their lack of resiliency is something to watch when working with children and movement. The teacher should restrict or eliminate falls and jumps because a hard, unyielding surface puts a lot of stress on developing joints and young bones. Children can be comfortable and safe sliding in a lying or sitting position, walking, or stretching on floors, such as smooth, painted concrete, that look uninviting to adults. Think about which activities are appropriate for your floor surface.

Many movement activities for children take place on the floor so you will want to consider its cleanliness and temperature for reasons of health and comfort.

Heat and ventilation. The temperature should be normal to cool in a movement activities area. The children will become warm quickly, and an overheated room is uncomfortable. It is always pleasant to have windows that open so that the teacher can directly control temperature and ventilation. Stuffy rooms are unpleasant and should be avoided.

Distractions. If there are massive distractions which cannot be controlled, look for another space. Material distractions can sometimes be covered, removed, or placed firmly off limits to the children. Distracting people such as passers-by and observers are more difficult to control. The teacher's and children's ability to behave freely can be seriously inhibited if other people are able to come into the space easily. The teacher must make a personal judgment as to how observers will affect her or his ability to teach without inhibition. Younger children are generally able to disregard observers easily. As children grow older, some become self-conscious and have real difficulty performing freely if others are watching.

Safety. The movement space must be physically safe. There should be no sharp corners to run into or splintery floors to sabotage feet or hands. Be aware of the dangers posed by corners, pillars, rough floors, expanses of glass, and concrete walls. Consider the results of a child crashing into any surface of the room. The teacher's awareness of danger may be sufficient to prevent accidents.

Scheduling

Time of day. Movement activities tend to generate energy,

which means that at any time of day movement activities will work, even before lunch or at the end of the day. A special activity, such as relaxation, may be done when children will be changing their focus from movement to another activity.

Length of time. There can be great flexibility in the amount of time set aside for movement. A seven- and eight-year-old group of children can handle a 1-hour session easily. Three-year-olds may do better with a 15-minute class once a day. Remember that dressing and undressing for movement activities also take time.

The teacher may choose to hold shorter sessions under these circumstances: when first beginning to teach movement classes, when the group must be very large, or if the children are very young. These situations demand a lot of teacher energy; it is better to limit their duration than to exhaust yourself with the experience.

Frequency of sessions. As in other subject areas the more frequent the exposure, the more comfortable all the participants become. Ideally, there should be some time set aside every day for movement activities.

Children's attire

Removing shoes and socks is essential—they are slippery. Removing them gives special attention to doing movement. It gives a closer feeling to the ground, the feet have greater movement potential, and it prevents serious injuries from accidental kicking. When the teacher removes her or his own shoes and socks, it is helpful to talk about how nice it feels to feel the floor with the feet. Some children may be resistant or their parents may have asked them not to remove their shoes. These cases should be decided individually. If children need the security of shoes, they should be allowed to wear them. This is often the case with younger children. If it is a parental direction, assure the child that you will talk with the parent and that you assume the responsibility for the shoe removal. Make sure, however, that you do talk with the parent and arrive at a mutually agreeable solution.

Tights can also be a problem. They are slippery on a smooth

surface, so ask children who wear tights to keep an extra pair of shorts at school that they can change into. Tights without feet are also an alternative.

Except for these considerations, regular school clothes will generally do well in movement classes. If girls are troubled by skirts scooting up or by long skirts that impede movement, ask them to wear trousers or shorts next time. Another possibility is to ask the children to keep a pair of shorts and a T-shirt at school which they can change into for movement. It may be necessary to send a note home to parents to ask for their cooperation.

General rules for children

In order to create and maintain an atmosphere that will allow for maximum freedom and concentration during movement activities, a few rules are necessary. These expectations will help children control themselves.

- Children should not wear or carry dangerous items.
- Children must not be allowed to deliberately hurt one another physically.
- Children must not be allowed to tease or ridicule one another.
- Children must come to where the teacher is upon hearing a prearranged signal or when the teacher asks them to.
- Children are expected to behave with an appropriate degree of commitment to the activities.
- Older children must obey the direction "Freeze!"

Props

Drums can be useful as a means of establishing a beat, or as a signal for the class to gather or to freeze in a shape. A hand-held drum is a flexible instrument that you can hold as you move among the children. If a drum is used, children will be anxious to try their hands at playing it; you should consider if and when this can be appropriate. For example, at the end of the class after children have put on their shoes they can each take a turn. Drums should also be made available at other times as a part of the children's music experience.

Voice. The teacher's voice can be the very best instrument. With your voice, you can mark a beat or make a signal for the children to gather. The voice can make sounds or say words to accompany movement. Various moods can be created by altering the volume of the voice and by playing with the quality of the sounds that come out. The voice is a part of the body. A teacher who is comfortable using voice as an accompaniment, not necessarily a musical accompaniment, can help the children feel free to use their voices to accompany their movements.

Music can be a rich addition to movement classes. Although this book is not about teaching music, in activities for three- and four-year-olds, songs are integrated into movement sessions as a way to bring the group together and as a rhythmic accompaniment for movement. There are some wonderful materials and programs built around the musical experience that are referred to in the Bibliography. It makes good sense to bring musical activities into movement sessions when appropriate.

Many teachers choose to use records during movement sessions. Because most of the activities offered in this book are spontaneous, records are generally not appropriate except to set a mood, perhaps for fantasy work or during relaxation. You should decide whether adding music will enrich the experience. If records are chosen, it is essential that equipment be immediately responsive to the need. Fumbling to put the record on, finding the right band, or waiting for the machine to warm up can critically damage the mood that has been created.

Playing records the teacher or children like during other parts of the day is of great value. Social dancing and just moving to music is a pleasure for many people and is certainly something to encourage. Before school, at lunch time, or for a break during the day, music can be a source of enrichment.

A *sheet or blanket* is a versatile prop for working with younger children. The children can be carried in it, they can roll up in it, and they can hide under it during fantasies.

The teacher's role

Dealing with the energy

In movement activities the energy level is often very high. It is important that, at times, a high energy be encouraged, but it is equally important that the teacher know how to control energy and bring it to focus on the activity. If this does not happen, the children sense a craziness which can be frightening. You must also be able to control the energy for your own sake. Teaching movement is tricky because of this high-energy element, and can be alarming to the teacher who has difficulty pulling the group back together. Grounding activities for the children should be used in these high-energy, out-of-control situations (p. 17).

Allowing for creativity

The teacher must deal swiftly and effectively with those situations where one child ridicules others. A quiet word and a serious look from the teacher may be enough to make it clear that such behavior will not be tolerated. If necessary, the child should be taken aside and spoken with firmly. Children who tease are surely fearful that someone will laugh at them if they move in an extraordinary manner so it is all the more important that all children understand no one is allowed to make fun of another in movement class, or anywhere else for that matter. In movement classes everyone is particularly vulnerable to ridicule because all are asked to take risks. Children are asked to demonstrate with body and mind a solution to a problem or an expression of feeling. Holding back inhibits the creative process, and children will surely hold back if they think someone might laugh at them. Movement classes must be emotionally safe.

The teacher must be careful not to take the creative process from the children. This is perhaps one of the greatest dangers in teaching any creative activity. You must constantly examine what is occurring to insure that the creative process lies with the students and not with yourself. For example, you ask the children to move from one point to another at the lowest level. You know that an efficient way of doing this is rolling, but you must let the children discover this. Or, you ask the children to be eggs on the ground and you have a mental picture of what an egg on the ground looks like. You *could* designate the shape you have in mind, but for the children to feel the freedom of creativity, you must let them choose the shape their own bodies should be in to mean *egg*. Always expect the children to be intelligent and creative. The results may not look the way an adult wants, but creativity is a process not a product. Help children always feel confident that their ability to find a solution is respected. All of the activities should build a framework within which children can exercise their creativity and intelligence. Your job is to see that the conditions are right for creativity and intelligence to emerge.

Providing support

The safe feeling in movement activities is best fostered by the teacher's support of creative efforts. You can express support through a smile or a touch of the hand; through respect for the space that the child is occupying (by not interrupting); through any acknowledgment of the contribution of a child (describing what was done without mentioning the child's name); or by privately discussing with a child after class the work that the child did within the class.

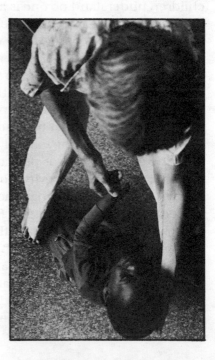

The hands of the teacher can guide and can assure the child that he is being cared for.

Your hands are a tool of nonverbal communication in working with children. They receive children after a difficult floor crossing; they identify the body part being talked about; they guide the child's body through a movement; they encircle the child as she or he tries a new and frightening activity. Your hands should be strong, kind, firm, and reassuring. The child being touched, and the observing child, both recognize the language your hands speak.

If a child does something of particular interest within a class, it may be important to point out what is happening in order to expand what other children are doing; however, it is important that there not be a qualitative note to the comment. For example, the teacher could say, "Oh, look. Ezra has found a way to get across the floor without using his feet at all," instead of "That is good, Ezra." Saying that one child's work is good may imply that other children's work is not good, or that the previous work that a child did was not good enough to warrant comment. The teacher wants to push children toward more creative solutions to problems and using a qualitative word such as *good* may not focus attention on variety; it may imply arrival at the only solution.

Often children will ask the teacher to look at what they are doing. If they do, it is then appropriate to say "Terriffic," "Good!" or another such qualitative, supporting word. A similar situation can occur if children are performing for one another. After each performance it is important that there be a positive comment on some aspect of the work, and qualitative words are again appropriate: "I liked the way Paul's body wrapped around George's so that they looked like one creature. That was wonderful!"

When the children are doing an activity, often one child will do an interesting variation. It makes good sense to pick up on that idea and to have the class try it out. In that way, you are making clear to the students that you are watching carefully, and that you not only approve of their originality, but encourage others to explore that idea.

If the children are doing an activity where the others are waiting their turn, ask them what the person did that was different from the others' movements. If it is similar to what was done before, it would be appropriate to say, "Paul liked what Veronica did so much he decided he wanted to do it too. Now let's see what Latressa does."

If a child falls while trying a new movement, you might consider stopping the class and asking the others to try the movement: "Ryan was trying to hop like a frog in a way that was different from everyone else's. It was very hard, but we can all try it, because I think it was a good idea and I would like to learn how to move like that myself." You will alleviate Ryan's embarrassment with this approach and, once again, convey to the children your appreciation of creative efforts.

Expression of support should be given for creative efforts, for cooperation, for expressions of feeling, and for all of the other positive elements we want to encourage in children.

Modeling

When teaching movement, it is necessary to become involved. Often the teacher has to show by example what is wanted. This is particularly important with younger children. It is absolutely essential that very young children see your body do what is wanted while you talk about it. Language is a new form of communication, and it is difficult for most very young children to visualize what the words describe unless you are simultaneously acting out the words.

When the teacher models an activity, the children will initially imitate the teacher's movement. The teacher should watch carefully for those who begin moving beyond the imitation. The teacher may then choose to encourage these children. In this way, children will feel free to move in their own creative way. Additionally, the teacher is able to direct the other children's attention to children as models. For example, the teacher demonstrates crawling across the floor. Tom walks on all fours, instead of crawling. The teacher may then choose to say, "Let's try Tom's way. Tom, show us again how you came."

Additionally, the children need to see that your attention and body are totally absorbed by what is going on in the class. They understand by the way your body and voice describe something that a total commitment is expected from them in dealing with the problem at hand. If there are other adults watching you work,

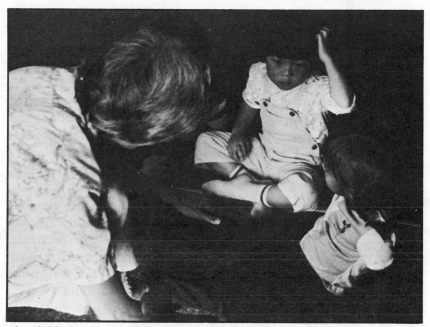

The child who watches develops confidence in the teacher as she works with others. This child speaks little English, and this was his way to learn about the activity.

your involvement may be half-hearted. Even as children are vulnerable during movement classes, so is the teacher. Become as involved as possible in what is happening so that you can respond appropriately and determine what should happen next. If the teacher is less than totally involved, the session will be more difficult; children will sense the teacher's distraction and will become distracted also.

Incorporating adult help

If you have another adult working with you during the movement session, there is a great deal you can do together to enhance the sessions. Review your plans for the session with your assistant and emphasize that you may deviate from the plan. Do not hesitate to give direction to your assistant during the session. Assistants appreciate knowing precisely how they can be most helpful. Your assistant will be most helpful to the children if she or he enthusiastically participates in activities as you direct. Assistants can accompany a shy child through an activity, assess the needs of the child who has an accident, show by the placement of their body where the children should come, or help develop the energy and concentration in the class because of their own involvement. Always emphasize to the assistant the child's right to watch, rather than participate, so that confrontations between child and assistant do not occur. During the session, pick up on the ideas of your assistant as well as on the ideas of the children.

At the end of the session, review what happened. Describe the discoveries you made and listen to the discoveries made by your assistant. Discuss what worked and what did not, why you made certain decisions, and what you plan to do during the next session based upon what occurred during this session. The more your assistant learns, the greater help she or he will be.

Finally, and of greatest importance, tell your assistants what you like about their work. Be specific, and be honest. Avoid criticism unless absolutely necessary, and then try to create a discussion on various ways to handle problems which cause you concern.

Pacing an activity

Before class begins, consider which elements to develop in an activity. Keep those elements in mind as you work; give the children time to discover the elements for themselves. There is a tendency to rush through activities with children to keep them busy. Instead, help them discover the subtle aspects of what is possible. Given time, as the activity proceeds, children will find new things that you had not thought of, to extend the activity in an entirely new way. If that direction is exciting, you may want to pursue its development. Or, if necessary, return to the elements you had in mind originally. The teacher always has a choice about direction and pace, but slowing down and allowing something new to happen or allowing children to dwell on something familiar for a moment is a choice not always recognized. Take your time. Enjoy the pace created by the activity.

Handling problems

The nonparticipant. In the first sessions there will almost certainly be some children who would rather not participate. A skilled assistant can be a great help by saying enthusiastically to the child, "That looks like fun. Let's do this one together!" and if the child resists, "That's fine. Maybe next time." Try to watch such a child until you notice interest in a particular activity and then try another invitation.

Participation should be strongly encouraged. However, if a child seems truly unable to take part, she or he should be asked to sit and watch quietly from the side. That child should not be allowed to bother the others or to return to other classroom activities because at some point, after observing for a good period of time or for several periods of time, the reticent child may be able to join the group again. Some younger children may need to observe the activities for quite some time until they believe that they will be safe if they participate. They may then choose to participate only in certain activities. Often the child who just watches will be absorbing an enormous amount which will emerge at some other time—or perhaps only at home. Older children should be expected to continue to the end once they have begun a class; they should not be encouraged to reject at whim what the teacher offers.

An out-of-control group. There are several ways to ground children.

1. Say "Freeze!" From the statue pose have children sit on the ground and spin on their buttocks.

2. Say "Freeze!" From the statue pose have children collapse instantly to the floor, rise slowly, and collapse again, as many times as is necessary to calm them. Begin focusing their attention on the shapes they are making on the ground.

3. Say "Freeze!" Move to another part of the room and have the children gather there, sitting on the floor ready for a new activity. It is often effective to bring the children into a very close group and to speak almost in a whisper as you describe the next activity.

Bringing the children to the ground has a calming effect. To achieve this, you are using a control word, *Freeze!*, and then moving the children to an activity on the ground where they are isolated from one another.

Moving younger children on to a new activity is generally an effective solution to a loss of focus. Between all activities with younger children it is wise to bring them to the floor while you give them instructions for the next activity. Very young children understand "Everybody sit down!" The teacher must go down to the floor too so that it is clear what is meant.

Silliness. Use your judgment. If the situation seems as if it might go out of control, move to another activity or refocus the activity the silliness is emerging from. Consider, however, allowing some silliness to take place. A little relaxed silliness is sometimes appropriate.

Another type of silliness may occur when you give an instruction such as, "Freeze in the highest shape you can," and an inventive child finds a table to climb onto. Rather than negate the inventiveness, you can acknowledge the cleverness and add to the next instruction, " . . . with both feet on the ground." The child may be testing the teacher's equanimity or the child may be testing the reaction to a different interpretation of a direction. Let children who think in challenging directions know that there is space for them in these activities.

At about five years of age, some children become silly because they feel self-conscious working in front of others. These children can generally do group work where attention is not focused on one person. When individual work or work in pairs is done, often the teacher can arrange to have the self-conscious child's eyes focused away from onlookers.

Roughness and ridicule. As mentioned earlier, deliberately hurting someone or interfering with another child's participation in the session must be strictly forbidden. Speaking with the offenders privately after the session is the most effective, long-range solution. However, at the time of the transgression, you may need to separate the child from the group promptly, giving the incident as little extra attention as possible so that you are offering no form of reward for the offensive behavior.

*　　*　　*

Many of the teaching sessions in this book contain directions written as conversation. *These directions are not intended for you to memorize and repeat verbatim.* Rather, they suggest a tone that you will want to set for the activity. To keep the session as natural and smooth as possible, you will want to refer to your list containing the order in which you wish to do the activities. Spontaneity and intense observation of children require that you attend only to the children.

Part II: A Movement Program for Three- and Four-Year-Old Children

Chapter 2: Techniques for teaching sessions for younger children

The activities in this book are designed for movement sessions directed by an adult. However, it is essential that these activities be only one portion of the total movement program for three- and four-year-olds. You will want to offer a variety of movement experiences in order to meet the needs of the children in your program. Some children have an enormous need to move and to use movement as their predominant mode of learning; others need to be encouraged to move. Some children will explore movement when they are alone and have no possibility of interference; others are drawn in by the activity of a group. Some children may have experienced a wide range of movement activities outside of the group and others may have had very little movement experience. There are many factors, but the important point is that movement activities need to be offered in varied contexts because children have differences in learning styles, personalities, and developmental levels.

A large portion of the knowledge children have acquired by the age of three has been through tactile and kinesthetic experiences—children know safety because of an adult's reassuring strokes; they know danger because fire hurts. Children reach out into the world with their bodies and learn that by moving in certain ways their position in space is altered, for example, turning onto the stomach after lying on the back. Kinesthetically children learn to alter the position of their bodies. Tactile and kinesthetic experiences are still very important modes of learning at three years of age. Because some children develop more rapidly than others, these are stronger modes of learning for some than for others.

Recently there has been an abundance of work in the field of learning disabilities (Ayres 1972—73; Kantner et al. 1976; Walsh and Greenough 1976). It has been found that tactile, kinesthetic, and labyrynthian stimulation are essential for normal brain development. Labyrynthian stimulation means that the inner ear mechanism is stimulated through such activities as rocking, balancing, and swinging. Adults are filling the child's need for labyrynthian stimulation when rocking a baby. The subject is complex, but for those of us involved in movement and early childhood education, this information is fascinating because it gives us insight into the behavior of children, and it assists us in planning a movement program.

Many children enjoy and all have an innate need for activities which involve tactile, kinesthetic, and labyrynthian stimulation. Thus, tactile activities such as cuddling a blanket and sand and water play are popular. Likewise, kinesthetic activities such as running and jumping, crawling and hopping are often successful. Labyrynthian activities such as swinging and rocking, twirling and balancing are attractive activities to some children. Consider these three factors when planning your total movement program.

However, it is essential to continually assess the needs of the individual child. Children's tolerance levels for these activities vary from day to day. The adult must respect each child's response to the offered activity. *Only a trained therapist is in a position to impose a given movement activity upon a child.*

Probably every program of movement for three- and four-year-olds includes body awareness. Often *body awareness* implies simply naming body parts, but for young children movement *is* body awareness. Children are learning what their bodies can do. They are continually developing new skills. They are defining the physical perimeters of their bodies. They are becoming less generalized and more specific in their recognition of where the different parts of their bodies are and what those different specific body parts can do individually or in union with other parts of the body. They are becoming aware of the body's movement range from frantic activity to rest. All of the movement activities for three- and four-year-olds in this book deal with the development of this body awareness.

The purpose of movement sessions

Movement for three- and four-year-old children has traditionally taken place in free play situations. Often music and some teaching of skills have complemented the free play. These activities continue to be necessary and important to the movement program. However, through movement sessions we are able to bring a group of children together in a more formal setting. We are able to encourage movement and emphasize its importance in the curriculum by having formal movement sessions.

Within these sessions, concepts are taught. The concepts are not taught rigidly, but through their recurrence over time. At the beginning of each activity or group of activities in this book, a concept or an objective is stated. The children will learn these concepts gradually over the course of the sessions. Each concept will appear repeatedly in different forms as you teach, and the concept will gradually become a part of the child. For example, being able to move backward while crawling will demand concentration the first few times but as the activity recurs in the classes, it will be done with greater ease, and the child will be more familiar with her or his backward space.

The movement session space

The group meeting space is often suitable if the nonparticipating children are engaged in activities elsewhere. If it is too small, you may need to push back tables. Children generally enjoy helping prepare the space. After the first session, taking off shoes and socks and preparing the space occur fairly easily because children are looking forward to the activities.

Determine your greatest distance in this space for the floor crossings (p. 60). About 15 feet is a good distance. At each end of this space, define an area where the children should sit while waiting their turn to cross. This can be defined with a line of masking tape on the floor, a chalk line, or carpet squares. There should be enough room at each end of the crossing space for the entire movement group to sit.

Active movement spaces

Most facilities for three- and four-year-olds have an outdoor space or an interior space that functions in much the same way as an outdoor space. If not, frequent trips to the park are usually an important part of the program because it is recognized that young children need to move in large ways. Every child needs to have unstructured, active play during the day.

Let's Play Outdoors (Baker 1966) is full of suggestions for inexpensively using an existing outdoor space. If you would like to do a major project to develop your outdoor space, there are several books available. *Play Structures: Questions to Discuss, Designs to Consider, Directions for Construction* (Ellison 1974) is a good source of ideas for structures. *Playing, Living, Learning: A Worldwide Perspective on Children's Opportunities to Play* (Westland and Knight 1982) explores many exciting possibilities for play yards including adventure playgrounds and naturalistic environments.

If you have a wild area available to you with trees and hills, fallen logs and ponds, places to hide in and to explore, and materials with which to create and to take apart and to recreate a nest or home or fort, you are most fortunate. Use wisely what you have. If you do not have such an area, you can attempt to replicate such experiences by enhancing the classroom's outdoor environment. Some of the equipment, materials, and activities which might be included in this area at various times during the year are listed here.

■ Sand, water, and soil. Tools for working in these materials. See Hill (1977).

■ Climbing structures with fire poles and places to hang by hands, arms, and legs. Places to develop arm strength are important.

■ Trees to climb and to hide in. Trees provide a special challenge and develop problem-solving and risk-taking skills.

If hiding places do not occur naturally in the play yard, children derive great pleasure from creating them.

■ Mats are very useful, if grass is not available, for tumbling activities such as rolling and somersaults. Informal relaxations and massages are lovely on mats. Use them also for the activities for one child and one adult working together in Part IV.

■ Inclined areas or hills on which to move and to take wheel toys.

■ Smooth surfaces to slide on, such as a hardwood floor.

■ A slide ending at a soft surface so that the child can come down feet first or head first, on back or stomach.

■ Straw to jump into or hide in.

■ Balls of various sizes and adults to teach their use. Bowling games are excellent. See Kamii and DeVries (1980) for information on group games.

■ Bean bags and targets for throwing. Adults usually need to help create the situation.

■ Ropes, with careful supervision, can be used for jumping and for dramatic play. A thick, knotted rope makes a new kind of swing and a new kind of climbing apparatus, both of which develop arm and hand strength.

■ Tricycles, wagons, scooters, and other wheel toys.

- Swings and hammocks.
- Tables covered with blankets to make houses or hiding places.
- Tires, planks, foam mattresses, ladders, large and small wooden boxes, sawhorses, blankets, and barrels that children can move with help and supervision to create climbing structures, obstacle courses, and dramatic play structures.
- Balance beams and bouncing boards.
- A large bag of fabric stuffed with fist-sized foam scraps (not shredded foam) that the children can jump onto, relax on, slide down into, or crawl over. The bag should be the size of two double bed sheets sewn together. Mogar (1980) calls these *bumpety bumps.*
- Cardboard boxes, both large and small. Children can use small boxes for sitting in, making trains, and other dramatic play activities.
- A place, perhaps a table, to jump from; a soft place, a mattress or a bumpety bump, by its side to jump onto.
- Large, hollow blocks.
- Props for dramatic play, such as toy cars, toy boats, capes, clothing, scarves, hobby horses, fire hoses, kitchen utensils, and other articles from the drama area.
- Obstacle courses.
- Paints, clay, and manipulative toys, or books. You can bring virtually any inside activity outside, weather permitting. This encourages the timid child to be outside and provides a place for such a child to observe more active events. Additionally, the physically active child may decide to participate in a different type of learning activity.
- Carpentry. Seven- to 13-ounce claw hammers and nails with large heads are best for young children. Recommended wood types are white pine, poplar, cedar, and spruce. The woodworking area should be carefully defined and supervised for maximum safety (Skeen, Garner, and Cartwright 1983).
- Science materials.
- Musical instruments.
- If you have studied yoga, do exercises, or like to jog or dance to contemporary music, by all means bring these activities into

class. Children are often fascinated by what you like to do, because you bring a strong knowledge and enthusiasm with your pastime.

■ Records. If you enjoy dancing, some children will probably join you, especially if you persist by frequently putting on dance records. Remember that if only one child joins you, the experience may be very important for that one child. Others may be too shy to join but vicariously join by watching. Records of children's songs and games are very appropriate to use with small groups of children during informal times of day.

Always be absolutely certain your high equipment has soft landing spaces underneath. Falling onto a hard surface can be fatal. Always provide adequate supervision of activities for safety.

When special materials are brought outside, it is important that children be expected to treat them with respect. Often the outdoors invites careless use of materials.

If there is a long winter where you live, consider which activities you can bring into the classroom from outdoors. You can furnish classrooms with pillows, mats, foam mattresses, small climbing structures, hanging knotted ropes, hammocks, and rocking toys so that children are not deprived of free choice movement experiences when outdoor play is not possible.

Playing with children

Another name for playing with children is movement improvisation. Among dancers, a common format for movement improvisation is deciding upon a framework and then moving within this framework. For example, if three people are doing a movement improvisation together, they might decide that each person must be at one of three levels: on the ground, in a middle level, or upright. No two people can be at the same level at one time. Players can change levels whenever they choose. Movement possibilities are infinite within this structure. The dancers must be aware constantly of each other's movement. It is a game, similar to many inventions of childhood, in which your body and mind are constantly challenged.

For some adults active play is the most natural activity in the world. For others it is difficult to take that first step back into childhood where we make believe and run and dodge and giggle, where we construct, in an instant, a movement improvisation framework and then drop it. At times we fear looking foolish and at others we seem to lack energy. Perhaps it just does not occur to us when we are supervising play that our role could be more active.

Playing with children is valuable because it provides us with another way of communicating with children. When you physically interact with a child your hands can say, "I care for you." When you climb up the Jungle Gym with a child, you are saying, "This is something I enjoy, too."

Being involved in physical activities with the children indicates graphically that you think physical activity and play are important. For the child who feels very comfortable in active play this means, "The teacher appreciates what I'm doing." For the child who feels more comfortable with sedentary activities, this means, "The teacher thinks physical activity is fun. Maybe I'll give it a try."

Playing with children is fun. Many times a grumpy, tired teacher is transformed into a happier person by play. Moving is healthy for adults and children. If you are not physically able to move vigorously, an enthusiastic spirit—mentally joining the children as they play—can be very effective.

These are some ideas for initially involving children in active play.

Games and singing games such as *"Ring Around the Rosy," "Little Sally Walker," "London Bridge," "Here We Go 'Round the Mulberry Bush,"* or *"Miss Mary Mack."* Any game the children know or the teacher knows can entice children to participate. Remember also the smaller individual games such as *"This Little Piggy Went to Market."* You might want to expand upon the original—for example, rolling onto your back and shoulders after you fall down in *"Ring Around the Rosy."*

Wrestling on mats or grass. There are two rules:

1. Only two people at one time.
2. When one person says, "Stop!" both people stop wrestling and separate.

The supervising adult can also wrestle with one child at a time. It is important to be sensitive to the child you are wrestling with and to allow that child to feel strength over you. Include a lot of body rubbing and rolling and do not let the child win too easily. If the child is on top of you and has your arms pinned down, you can match your efforts to the child's strength so that the child really has to work to keep you there.

Alternatives to walking. When you go somewhere, go differently. You can hop, walk backward, jiggle all over, whatever strikes your fancy.

Make-believe. Go on a trip, have a picnic, celebrate a birthday, take somebody to the hospital, act out "The Three Billy Goats Gruff" or other stories—these ideas are a diversion from the superhero fantasies which are so strong with many children. You will not have a shortage of ideas for fantasies because children are so creative. Be careful to not take over the fantasy; you need to go along with the children's ideas as much as possible. Children enjoy doing the same fantasies over and over. You and your group of children will develop your own personal stories.

Tumbling. Roll and somersault together. Practice headstands and handstands. Usually some of the children can do amazing cartwheels. Admire them and encourage them to do cartwheels on both sides of their bodies. The somersault is a basic skill most children develop at this age. The child should tuck the head completely through her or his arms so the *back* of the head and the top of the back touch the floor first, *not* the crown. Help the children learn by having them somersault over your knee or your shoulder (see Part IV).

Play on mats or grass. Try the activities for one child and one adult from Part IV.

Books. Bring out a book to read together. Then put it down and act it out. *Caps for Sale* (Slobodkina 1940) is a favorite for this activity. Another kind of book is one like *Be A Frog, A Bird, or A Tree: Creative Yoga Experiences for Children* (Carr 1973). With this book, anyone can try different yoga postures.

Play on the equipment. Climb the Jungle Gyms, try the fire poles, see if you can hang by your hands, or even skin the cat!

Run around. One teacher finds "if the children are really high when they come to school, I just go out in the yard with them,

and we run around for awhile. Then everyone's OK." After you
run, you can gallop, skip, slide, or crawl. Children of this age do
not really need a destination. You can run in circles or from one
wall to another. You can have races to the fence in which everyone wins.

Imitate movement. Imitating a child's movement is a very sensitive thing to do. You must *never* make fun of the child. The
reflection of movement is a way of saying, "I appreciate that
movement. I want to try it." If you have guessed correctly about
the child and the situation, the child will do more movements for
you to imitate.

Games like tag and hiding. Modify the game to the level of the
children. In tag, whoever is IT can jump from one person to the
other depending on who wants to be IT.

For an adult, playing is letting go and joking around, remem-
bering what it was like to be very young. Even though you are
playing with children you are maintaining the role of adult. You
sometimes need to move quickly to a controlling position to
intercede if someone is about to be hurt. Children must always
know that you are still in charge or the situation may become
frightening. Although play is often active, when it becomes quiet
and gentle it is important that the teacher respect those moments. They should be treasured.

When an adult plays with children, it is necessary that the
children respect the adult's body. Many children like to jump on
an adult's back. This is shocking and sometimes painful. Children must quickly understand that you like to play, but that you
are the one to define in what ways you play.

When you first begin playing with children, you may be
swamped with children who are eager to take part. You are a
novelty, and you are also creating situations which many children enjoy. This situation can be similar to having one bicycle for
20 children. One way to deal with this problem is to keep a list of
the children who would like to participate. Be clear about who is
on the list. Write the children's names so that they can read them,
or let them write their own names, and read the list for them so
they are assured of their places. If you cannot work with everyone on the list during the time you have allotted, gather the
children who have not played with you and tell them you will

return tomorrow with the list and read the names once again. Limit the number of activities you do with the individual child. Consider giving the child a choice about which activities you do together. Talk with co-workers about what you are doing so they can understand the needs of the waiting children and can plan other activities. Another approach is to take 5 children to a private area and to do the activities with those 5 children in turn.

At times, it is appropriate for the teacher to step back and to spend a period of time observing the activities in the space. What are the children doing? Who is consistently outside the activity? How can the arrangement of equipment and materials be improved? Is there enough supervision? Taking time out to observe is necessary in order to be certain that the environment supports the growth of your children.

How many children?

If possible, limit the number of children you work with at one time to about 10. It is helpful to have one adult assistant with this number of children. It is possible to do the sessions without an assistant, but it is more difficult. If a special problem arises with 1 child, you may lose the attention of others while you tend to that child. If you do not have an assistant, choose activities in which the whole group can always be actively involved or in which waiting time for each child's turn is brief. As an alternative you can limit the group to 5 to 7 children.

Shoes and socks

Determine ahead of time where shoes and socks will go. Be certain to show children how to put their socks in their shoes at the first session. As mentioned earlier, do not insist that children take off their shoes and socks. Some children really *need* to keep their shoes on. However, after you take your own shoes off, you can rub the soles of your feet on the floor and talk about how nice it feels to encourage movement in bare feet.

Planning a session

For each session, think about what the children did at the previous session. Is there something you would like to develop more fully? Did the children make a request you did not have time to try? Did your assistant have an idea you did not have time to pursue? Build your next session around these ideas.

If someone makes a request when you begin a session, consider accommodating the request, but also feel free to tell the person you are postponing the requested activity until the next session. When you do the activity, mention who requested it. This makes clear to the group that you are interested in what they want, and gives them some control over the material.

When you begin a session, choose an activity that brings the group together and focuses attention upon you as the leader. Children need to listen to you and to watch you for direction. During the first moments of the session you can establish control as the children focus on you. The songs and activities in the section on bringing the group together (p. 39) establish your role and the group feeling. Most of these activities are not too strenuous. Because children will move vigorously during the session, a warming up activity (p. 52) should follow. If the group is very restless, move quickly to a warming up activity so that the children can use up some of their energy and then concentrate on subsequent activities chosen from movement and body awareness (p. 59), strength and groundedness (p. 71), trust and sensitivity (p. 83), or fantasy (p. 92). If the group is young you can hold a shorter session, choosing perhaps only two activities and then ending the session (p. 96). When you hold your first sessions with a group or if it is early in the year and the children do not know one another well, choose activities that focus more heavily on movement and body awareness or fantasy. Strength and groundedness or trust and sensitivity activities work well if children know the teacher and each other. If the session can run longer than 30 minutes, select beforehand at least four activities to do before your ending activity. The final activities are generally relaxed so that children are able to move back into the classroom calmly.

At times, movement teachers may be in the middle of a session and not have any idea what should happen next. For a safeguard, write down activities planned for a session in an order you hypothesize will work. When you do lose your train of thought, bring the children to the floor to end the activity. Then you can glance at your list, decide what you want to have happen next, and move on. If the children are grounded, they will stay on the floor for a moment or two while you plan the next activity.

Pacing the session

The pace of sessions for three- and four-year-olds is fairly brisk. The children need to move quickly from one kind of movement to another. This does not mean that the movements themselves need to be quick, but that one does not spend a long period of time doing one kind of movement. There are always exceptions. For example, if you incorporate a Zuni Rain Dance into a session, the repetition of movement is a strong part of the dance. If you have a focused group of children, they can do the same movement over and over so that the feeling of that repetition has meaning for them. Prolonged repetition is an unusual circumstance, however, for this age group.

Children of this age enjoy repeating certain activities day after day. Running, jumping, rolling, crawling, galloping, spinning, to name a few, will recur again and again.

When teaching movement, always work with contrasts. Contrast fast movements with slow movements, difficult movements with easy movements, up in the air with down on the floor, looseness with tightness, or big movements with little movements, for example. Contrast keeps everyone involved.

Using your voice

Language should be an integral part of movement work with young children. Simple words can describe the activity the child is performing. "Run. Run. Run. Run. Stop. Down on the ground goes Freddy." Repetitions are essential. In addition to the language-learning effect, repetitions create a beat for children to move by. The teacher should repeat the words at the same point in the movement every time a child does the movement. Voice helps the movement along and involves more of the child's body because the ears and the mind also become part of the movement. The energy of the class can be working with the child who is moving. When one child is performing, the other children can become a supportive chorus. When the whole group is moving, the teacher's voice is a supportive chorus.

To move and to make sounds at the same time is difficult. The younger chidren are, the less able they are to say or sing words while moving.

Using the child's name often provides reassurance and recognition for that child. The teacher can repeat the child's name as the child moves or is being moved. Use the child's name in the song if possible. A name is a familiar sound that has great meaning for each of us.

Teaching the session

Teaching a movement session to three- and four-year-olds can be a vigorous activity for the teacher. You can regard it as a way to keep in shape. Sometimes one of the children can model an activity as you explain it or you can ask a child to repeat a movement that she or he did spontaneously so that others may try it. However, to keep things moving and to demonstrate what you want, you will have to spend a good part of the session doing the movement with the children. You will find this fun and invigorating. Children are usually very enthusiastic about activities if the teacher is.

Although you will have some days where everything goes wrong and everything you try becomes scattered, remember that you are learning the art and skill of teaching movement. Keep a journal of what you do, and you will discover as you reread it that you have learned an enormous amount. As you become more confident as a teacher of movement you will find much satisfaction in your own knowledge, the growth you see in children, and the shared joy of moving with children.

A first-session plan

With young children, particularly, it is important that the children know you and trust you before you leap into very strenuous activities. Very exciting activities can overwhelm, frighten, or overstimulate some children. They may come from homes where physical activity is minimal or nonexistent or where running and jumping is not possible. Adults doing these activities may seem very strange. A feeling of calm and control in the sessions eases the transition to these activities. Song games provide a transition—particularly during the warming up activities which need to be stimulating enough to get the blood flowing.

Keep the first session short—perhaps only three or four activities. Your purpose during this session is to teach the routine and the structure of the sessions, and to give the children a glimpse of the kinds of activities they will do.

Begin the session with a song familiar to the children. Then move to one that has some action possibilities such as *"Clap, Clap, Clap Your Hands"* for warming up. First, clap your hands; then do these movements in turn: pat your knees, rub your arms, touch your nose, crawl around, walk on your knees, jump up and down, jiggle all over, turn around, jump up and down (again), rub your legs, wash your hair, jump up and down (again), and sit back down. Then begin an activity from the movement and body awareness section, such as a floor crossing. Perhaps choose wriggling across on the belly like a lizard or snake for the first crossing. Depending upon your space, send the class all at once, or in groups of five. Next, the group can go one by one for the second crossing—talk about each child's movement as she or he wriggles across. Everyone can crawl back across together for the third crossing and then crawl backward in pairs for the fourth crossing.

Make certain the children sit in the designated spot after they have crossed the floor. For the individual crossings, either you or your assistant should sit on the side the children are moving toward. As each child arrives, the adult can pat the floor to indicate where the child should sit. If you have no assistant, sit on the side the children are moving toward, call the children by name, make comments to the other children about what the performer is doing, and pat the spot where you would like the child to sit upon arrival.

After floor crossings, you will probably choose an activity to end the first movement session. A brief relaxation would be appropriate. Ask each child to find a space where she or he can lie belly down. When you rub each child's back briefly, talk quietly to the child and tell her or him, "This is your back I am touching. All of this is your back." Run your hands all along the back. "You did good work today. It's time to start putting on your shoes." Your assistant can help with the shoes and socks. If you have no assistant, the children can begin by themselves with you joining them to help when you finish touching everyone.

A first session such as this one may last 30 minutes.

Field trips

Often the most successful field trips with three- and four-year-olds involve movement experiences. The school's location determines which field trips are feasible. Consider what you have available within easy walking distance. A trip to a grassy slope where the class can play freely and then eat a snack or lunch before returning to school is simple and yet provides a sound physical activity.

Walk as much as possible. Repeating routes so that there are certain landmarks and experiences to look forward to, such as walking on a ledge, breaks the tedium of getting to a place. Walking is a healthy habit which you can develop in children.

Here are some suggestions for field trips that provide special kinds of physical experiences. All of these locales can move beyond the physical experience to become the background for science investigations, art projects, or whatever the teacher plans or the class discovers. However, the pure physical experience of moving around in these spaces has a great value which we need to appreciate.

Hills are wonderful for climbing, rolling down, running down, sliding down, lying on.

Sand dunes are wonderful for climbing, rolling down, sliding down, lying on, and also digging in.

The ocean and beach. The vastness and power of this setting is an awesome physical experience. Tidepool areas provide many physical challenges, in addition to the thrills of environmental discovery.

Swimming. Some schools include swimming as a part of their program. Check with your local recreation department, YWCA/YMCA, and community centers to see what you can arrange. Often parents are willing to pay a small amount or to raise money to provide this valuable experience for their children.

The shoreline of lakes, bays, and rivers. The terrain adjacent to shorelines is often varied and fascinating to explore. This is a good place for children to throw rocks—an activity which many children love but which is seldom safe to do.

A creek. Because of the shallowness of the water, danger is diminished. Children can spend hours wading; feeling water and mud around their toes, feet, and legs; building dams; improvising boats; and discovering.

A large expanse of grass. This is a place for lots of running. Ball play, parachute games, wrestling, quiet activities, rolling around, and circle games number among activities well-suited to grass.

A rough field is a challenge to talk or to run through. There are many opportunities for science explorations here.

A wooded area. Usually there are places to crawl through, climb over, balance on, and explore. Like the ocean, a wooded area has a special atmosphere to be savored.

Snow and ice. These provide unique body experiences.

Boulders and rocks. Climbing possibilities are the attraction but the hardness of the surfaces can be an impressive tactile experience.

A smooth-floored hallway or room. Skating in socks is challenging, and learning to run and then release your body into a slide is a sophisticated skill.

Piles of straw. Free-falling into a pile of straw is a unique experience. Few of us have this opportunity.

Many of these experiences are available to those of us who live and work in urban areas through trips to various parks and industrial areas in cities. However, some activities are more difficult to arrange. Often, family trips to some of these special places, such as tobogganing hills or sand dunes, can bring the school community together as the fundraising and the actual event take place.

In terms of safety, each place poses its own particular needs for supervision. Water is an especially alluring, silent danger. Very close adult supervision is essential around water. Each adult should be responsible for no more than two children.

Before each trip, every child should receive a name tag with the phone number of someone who will be near the phone. Assign each adult on the trip responsibility for certain children in order to allow maximum flexibility. Small groups can explore places much more easily than large groups, and small groups are much easier to manage. It is important that the adults understand which children are their responsibility and what the responsibility entails. It is also important that children know exactly which adult is their leader. The teacher can keep a master list of groupings but should be free to explore with a small group of children, too. Before people separate, determine a meeting time and place and rules appropriate for the event.

Chapter 3: Movement sessions for three- and four-year-old children

The activities for three- and four-year-olds are divided into seven sections and are arranged in an approximate order of difficulty within each section.

Bringing the group together

Singing a song or playing a circle game familiar to the children when they first come to movement sessions is a good way to make a smooth transition to this new activity. The children can sit on the floor in a familiar group setting where everyone knows words, melodies, and actions well. The teacher can use songs which have a movement element during the beginning of the session, unless a child has a special request. In that case, the group can sing the child's song first.

This book contains a sampling of useful songs and games. Every teacher constantly collects new songs and games; those listed here should be added to every movement teacher's list. *Songs to Grow On* (Landeck 1950) and *American Folksongs for Children* (Seeger 1948) are excellent sources of song games, as are the records of Ella Jenkins and Pete Seeger. Each culture has its own traditional songs and games; the teacher should use these within the class. Families can be a good source of material for this though often people need to be reminded before the games return to their memories. All of these songs and games are effective for a change of pace within the class also.

At times the children will be so full of energy at the beginning of the session that it is best to go immediately to a warming up activity. The games and songs are total group activities and are fairly closed; that is, they are done within a set structure and without latitude for individual choices except in a very limited way. As a result they provide a good contrast to other activities which are more individualistic and open, activities in which children make choices about the movements or sounds they use.

Most, but not all, of these songs and games are done in a circle. Children can form a circle by joining hands, letting go, and sitting down or by sitting on a drawing of a large circle on the floor. If the circle is going to move as part of the activity, indicate direction with your hand and arm.

When you introduce a game or song, repeat it at least three times so that the children begin to become familiar with it. Be certain to repeat the games several times on subsequent days. Children love to repeat games like *"Ring Around the Rosy"* and *"Jack/Jill in the Box"* so be prepared to play these very simple games at least three times before you move on to another activity.

Specific objectives identify key skills that children will focus on during each activity suggested in this book. General objectives for bringing-the-group-together activities are to work as a group, to listen for word and sound clues, and to have a good time.

"Open, Shut Them"

Objective: To coordinate verbal direction with body movement.

Consideration: This works well with younger children.

Directions: Everyone sits on the floor.

C   E   D low G C   E   D low G C D E   F   G
Op - en. Shut them. Op - en. Shut them. Give a lit - tle clap.
Open hands. Form fist.   *Clap hands.*

C   E   D low G C   E   D low G   G   F   E   D
Op - en. Shut them. Op - en. Shut them.   Put them in your
                                          Bring hands down to

C   C   E   D low G C   E   D low G   C D
lap. Creep them. Creep them. Gent - ly creep them.   Right up
lap. *Creep hands up to chin.*   *Hold fingers*

E   F   C   C   E   D low G C   E   D   E   G   F
to your chin. Op - en wide your lit - tle mouth. But do not
on chin.   *Open mouth wide.*   *Repeat.*   *Build tension.*

let them in.
Rush hands from chin to behind back.

Notes: This song should be sung two or three times the first time it is done. Very young children may not sing the song at all but just do the motions with you.

"Ring Around the Rosy"

Objectives: To learn the structure of a circle game. To feel the floor on your back.

Consideration: This works well with younger children.

Directions: "Everyone join hands. Let's make a circle. Now let's go around this way." Indicate with your hand and arm the direction in which the circle will move.

   C   C   A   D C   A A C   C   A D C   A
Ring   a - round the   ro - sy. A pock - et   full   of po - sies.
Walk around in a circle.

A simple circle game is a good device for bringing a group of two-year-olds together.

  C   A C   A   A C   C low F
Ash - es, ash - es, we all fall down.
Let go of hands and fall down together.

Extensions: Rolling onto your back is very natural.

Older children like to roll up onto their shoulders into a backward roll.

Roll onto your back, bring knees part of the way to the chest, and kick your bent legs from the knee down.

———————

Reprinted with permission from *What Shall We Do and Allee Galloo!* by Marie Winn, © 1970 Harper & Row.

"Jack/Jill in the Box"

Objective: To listen for the cue to pop out.

Considerations: A drum is useful. This works well with younger children.

Directions: "Let's all get down on the floor like this." Curl up with your knees on the floor and your head down. "That's good. Now look up for a minute. I am going to sing a song, and when you hear me clap my hands like this," (sharply clap your hands) "I want all of you to pop up out of your boxes. Now listen to the song."

  F C C   C F D D D   D C   C C   D E F
Jill is hid - ing down in her box. Won't some - one op - en the lid?
Children curl up on the floor with their heads down so that they cannot see you.

CLAP!
Everyone pops up into a kneeling position.

"Let's do it again." Repeat the song using *Jack* and *him* instead of *Jill* and *her*.

Extension: Vary the length of time children wait to hear the clap.

"Old Lady Sally"

Objective: To move from vigorous activity to calmness in response to verbal clues.

Consideration: This works well with younger children.

Directions: "I would like everyone to sit down and listen, and watch me. I am going to sing a new song for you."

low G G   G G   G   B   B   D   B low G   A   low F#
 Old   La - dy Sal - ly wants to jump - ty jump, jump - ty

    D   B   A low G   low G   G   G G   G low G A
 jump, jump - ty jump.   Old   La - dy Sal - ly wants to
Jump and jump and jump.

    D   B low G   low G A   A   A   B   B   A   A
 jump - ty jump.   And Old La - dy Sal - ly wants to
                    Bow deeply from the waist so that fingers touch

low G
bow.
the ground. Do not bend knees.

"Now everyone stand up and let's all bow together. I want to see some nice low bows. Good. Now let's all do the song together."

Extensions: Each child can do this in turn, with the teacher using the child's name instead of Sally.

Other motions can be used instead of jumping.

Note: This is also a good activity for ending a session because of the settling effect of the bow. I learned this game from Maggy Ginet who adapted and arranged it from *Ring Games Alabama* (Folkways Record #7004).

Lyrics reprinted with permission from *Negro Songs from Alabama* by Harold Courlander, © 1960 by Harold Courlander. Music notations as given here are based on original transcriptions as they appear in *Negro Songs from Alabama* by Harold Courlander, © 1960 by Harold Courlander.

Body Part Hello

Objective: To isolate the movement of specific body parts.

Consideration: This activity is very brief.

Directions: "Let's say hello with our hands." Everyone waves both hands. "Now let's do the other arm and hand. Now let's do both arms and hands. Can you wave only your arm and not your hand?" Continue, using other body parts such as head, shoulders, feet, legs, knees, elbows, or back.

"Head, Shoulders, Knees, and Toes"

Objectives: To identify different parts of the body. To coordinate movement with words.

Directions: Everyone should be sitting down. "I am going to teach you a new song. Now watch and listen carefully."

G A G   F   E F   G   D   E   F   E   F G
Head and shoul - ders, knees and toes. Knees and toes. Knees and toes.
Touch designated parts of the body with both hands.

G A G   F   E   F   G G D D   G   G E C
Head and shoul - ders, knees and toes. We all clap hands to - geth - er.
Clap hands several times.

"Let's do it together."

Extensions: Older children are challenged by going very quickly, and are fascinated by going very slowly with a big, deep voice.
    Hum the tune. No words.
    Mouth the words silently.

Notes: The tune for this version is "London Bridge Is Falling Down." There is another version where you touch "eyes and ears and mouth and nose." I prefer this version for three- and four-year-olds, because clapping hands at the end provides a release from the concentration of the first part of the song.

———————

Lyrics reprinted with permission from *Do Your Ears Hang Low?: 50 More Musical Fingerplays* by Tom Glazer, Doubleday, 1980. © 1980 by Tom Glazer.

"Little Sally Walker"

Objectives: To listen to and to follow dramatic directions. To establish a pattern of giving support to the central performer.

Considerations: Every child who wants to should have an opportunity to be in the middle. This can be solved by several children being in the middle at one time, though traditionally there is just one Sally.

Directions: "Let's hold hands and make a circle. Now everyone sit down, listen to the song, and watch what I do."

G   G   E   A   G   E G   G   E A   G   E
Lit - tle Sal - ly Walk - er   sit - ting   in   a   sau - cer.
Squat.   *The rest is spoken.*

R - i - s - e, Sally, r - i - s - e
Stand up slowly.

And wipe your weeping eyes. Put your hands on your hips
Wipe eyes.   *Put hands on hips.*

And let your backbone slip.

Shake it to the East. Shake it to the West.
Shake hips and speed up the words.

Shake it to the one that you like the best.

"Let's all do it together now."

Extensions: This song is really a circle game with one child in the center and the others walking around in a circle until the central child rises. I then have everyone join in the rest of the actions up to the end.

If the central figure is a boy, you can say *Sammy Walker* instead of *Sally Walker*.

Substitute the child's name for *Sally Walker*.

Words and music by Bessie Jones. Collected and edited with new material by Alan Lomax. TRO—© Copyright 1972 Ludlow Music, Inc., New York, N.Y. Used by permission.

"Looby Loo"

Objective: To isolate the movement of just one body part.

Directions: "Today I'd like to teach you a song I used to sing when I was a child. We need to be in a circle. Everyone take hands and let's make a circle together. Now put your hands on your legs and listen."

C   C   C   E   C   G   C   C   C   E   C   D   C   C   C
Here we go loo - by loo. Here we go loo - by lye.   Here we go

E   C   G   G A G F   E   D   C
loo - by loo. All on a Sat - ur - day night.

Before going on to the second verse, ask children to join you. "All right, let's take hands and sing our song while we walk around in a circle in this direction." Indicate with your hand and arm the direction toward which the circle should move. Sing the song and move in a circle. "Good. Now the second part of this song goes like this."

C   C   C   E   C   G C C   C   E   C   D
I   put my ha - and in, I put my ha - and out,
Put hand and arm toward center of circle, then outside circle.

C   C   C   E   C   G   G   G   G   G   F   E D   C
I   give my hand a shake, shake, shake, and turn my - self a - bout.
Shake hand and arm vigorously. Turn body around.

"Let's do it together." Do the second part of the song with the motions. "And now we do the first part of the song again. Everyone take hands and let's go." Repeat the first verse again. Alternate the circle chorus with the action verse. Actions include: hand, other hand, foot, other foot, head, whole body.

Extensions: I do not use *right hand* or *left hand* until the children are old enough to make this differentiation. This is a good preliminary activity because a differentiation is made with *other*.

_____

Lyrics reprinted with permission from *Do Your Ears Hang Low?: 50 More Musical Fingerplays* by Tom Glazer, Doubleday, 1980. © 1980 by Tom Glazer.

"Mulberry Bush"

Objectives: To act out various activities. To think about work and to devise a representative action for a given job.

Directions: "Everyone take hands and let's make a circle. We're going to learn a new game. Listen to the first part of the song."

| C | C | C | C | E | G | G | E | C | C | D | D | B | low G |

Here we go 'round the mul - ber - ry bush, the mul - ber - ry bush,

low C G G E C C C C E G G E C

The mul - ber - ry bush. Here we go 'round the mul - ber - ry bush,

C D D low G G C C

so ear - ly in the morn - ing.

"Let's sing that and we'll walk around in a circle in this direction." Indicate with your hand and arm the direction toward which the circle should move. The movement of the circle should be lively. "Good. Now the second part of the song goes like this. You can do it with me."

C C C C E G͡G E C   D B low G G   E C
This is the way we sweep our house, sweep our house, sweep our house.
Use a motion that can be easily repeated.

C C C C E G͡G E C C D D low G G   C   C
This is the way we sweep our house, so ear - ly   in   the morn - ing.

"And now take hands and we go around in a circle again." Repeat song.

Extensions: Continue using the traditional activities such as "wash our clothes, dry our clothes, iron our clothes, make our bread." Then ask the children which activities they think they should do. Some suggestions I have been given are grocery shop, back pack, drive our car. Savor the contrast between the activity and the circle walk.

Note: This can be a beautiful time to talk about the different kinds of work that people do.

_____

Lyrics reprinted with permission from *Eye Winker, Tom Tinker, Chin Chopper: Fifty Musical Fingerplays* by Tom Glazer, Double-day, 1973. © 1973 by Tom Glazer.

Names

Objectives: To create a group feeling. To use the voice as part of the movement. To be able to move in a tight group without collisions.

Considerations: This activity is appropriate for four-year-olds but would be difficult for three-year-olds.

Directions: "I want everyone to join me here in a small circle. Come in close. Everyone squat like I am. Now watch me." Count

Names *is a particularly good game for creating an intimate group feeling.*

to 10 slowly and steadily. Clap your hands as you say every number. When you reach 10, jump into the air, shout your name, and come back quickly to your original position with your palms flat on the ground. "What we are going to do is count to 10. When we reach 10, jump into the air, shout your name, and then get back down to the ground as fast as you can. Hit the ground with your hands when you get back down. Are you ready?"

Extensions: Say different words, like *hamburger,* or *taco.* If it is someone's birthday, say that person's name.

Shout the name in a whisper.

Notes: Repeat this activity at least three times. Emphasize that children must return to the floor as quickly as possible; otherwise they begin to fly away from the group. If you feel the class can repeat the activity as many times as you have children in the group, the entire group can shout each child's name. It is important, if the group does one child's name, that every child in the group have an opportunity to hear her or his name shouted by the group.

Warming up

The activities in this section are group frameworks for vigorous activity. Except for *"Five Little Monkeys,"* all of them provide opportunities to explore a wide range of movements. A great deal of movement and body awareness work can take place within these frameworks. The warming up activities can be the core of your class, and can continue almost as long as you choose because interest remains high throughout. To maintain interest, always remember to contrast activities: difficult/easy, high/low, fast/slow, big/little, tight/loose.

Many young three-year-olds have difficulty freezing into a still position and so "Everybody sit down!" becomes the control phrase for these children.

If you introduce an activity that works fairly well, you should repeat it at the next meeting so that the children come to know the form. There is a comfort in familiarity, and knowing what to expect from the form frees a child to concentrate on the content. Younger children, especially, need more frequent repetitions to develop trust in the situation.

Opportunities for original movement occur within these activities. The teacher must be alert to spot the child's extension of the material so that that child's original movement can be shared with other children.

Specific objectives are given with each activity. General objectives for warming-up activities are to warm up the body and mind, that is, to get the heart beating and the blood flowing in order to loosen the muscles and stimulate the brain; to be able to move with other children without collision; to feel a personal creativity; to explore various locomotions and movements and to learn their identifying names.

"Five Little Monkeys"

Objectives: To move vigorously but with control. To move rapidly through the dramatic actions.

Consideration: This works well even with three-year-old or younger children.

Directions: "Let's see how many children we have today. Let's count." Touch each child as you count. "1, 2, 3, 4, 5, 6. We have six children. We are going to do a song called 'Six Little Monkeys' because we have six children, and you are all going to be the monkeys. This is how the song goes:"

(chant)	
Six little monkeys jumping on the bed.	*Jump up and down vigorously.*
They all fell down	*Fall down on the ground.*
and bumped their heads.	*Touch your head to the ground.*
Mama called the doctor,	*Hold pretend phone to ear.*
and the doctor said,	*Put one hand on hip and waggle the other hand as though scolding.*
"No more monkeys jumping on the bed."	

"Now, let's all try it together."

Extension: The last line can be delivered in a shout or in a whisper.

Note: Younger children love this game, particularly the last line where everyone gets to scold.

Races

Objectives: To move quickly. To avoid collision.

Considerations: There should be a clear wall (perhaps padded with mats) that the children can run and gently hit. This works well with younger children.

Directions: "I would like everyone to come to this end of the room with me. Now we are going to have a running race from here to that wall. When you get to that wall, hit it with your hands— but not so hard it hurts. Are you ready? Go." Run to the other wall. "OK, now we're going to run back the other way. Are you ready? Let's *go*." Run back. "OK. This time let's run backward carefully, like this. Be sure you watch to stop before the wall." Demonstrate for a few steps. "Are you ready? Let's go."

Extensions: Any form of locomotion can be used, for example, skipping, galloping, cross-over walks. Because this is a warm-up, the emphasis should be on quick movements.

Notes: Winning never even needs to enter in. If someone says, "I won," you can say, "Did anyone else win?" or just smile at the child in acknowledgment.

Everybody Sit Down

Objectives: To understand the phrase "Everybody sit down" as a signal to go down to the ground. To move vigorously and then stop.

Considerations: This activity is for young three-year-olds. *Freeze!* (p. 56) is a similar activity designed for older children. You will need a drum for this activity.

Directions: "When I hit the drum, move with me. When I hit the drum hard like this and say, 'Everybody sit down,' everyone should go down on the floor with me." Walk and hit the drum for each step you take. Say "walk" on every beat of the drum. After about 10 beats, hit the drum hard and say, "Everybody sit down" and fall to the ground. "Good. Now let's try it again." Repeat what you just did and this time more of the children should join you. Use running the next two times and then move to some other kinds of movement either from the list below, that you see a child doing, or that you suggest.

Extensions: Other movements that you can do with a younger group include crawling, walking backward, slow walk, fast walk, tip-toe walk, jumping, squatting walk, high-knee walk, big steps, tiny steps, frog jumps, jiggly walk, and stiff walk. Be certain to vary the difficulty. Intersperse running often because it requires less concentration for locomotion; children lose interest without some relief.

"Clap, Clap, Clap Your Hands"

Objectives: To follow verbal directions. To think up new movements. To identify body parts while touching them.

Directions: No words are necessary to introduce this song. It is self-explanatory. The children should be sitting down.

C   C   G   F   E   C   C   D   E   D low G
Clap, clap, clap your hands. Clap your hands to - geth - er.

C   C   G   F   E   E   E   D   D   C   C
Clap, clap, clap your hands. Clap your hands to - geth - er.

Continue, moving from sitting activities to more active locomotion.

Extensions: Suggestions for sitting: tap your knees, tap your elbows, tickle your toes, rub your legs, rub your arms, wash your hair, jiggle all over, bump up and down, scratch your arms, blink your eyes, shake your head, wave your arms. Use the suggestions for in-place movements (p. 63) and floor crossings (p. 60) for locomotions. Be certain to ask the children for ideas after you have done about four verses.

Notes: This activity is excellent as a first activity on those days when children are very high and cannot settle down for a song or circle game. It is also a good first activity for children new to movement.

Reprinted with permission from *American Folk Songs for Children* by Ruth Crawford Seeger, Doubleday, 1948. © 1948 by Charles and Ruth Seeger.

Freeze!

Objectives: To learn the meaning of "Freeze!" To move vigorously and stop on cue. To feel a creative power.

Considerations: This activity is most appropriate for four-year-old children. Use *Everybody Sit Down* (p. 54) with younger children. A drum is used for this activity.

Directions: "I would like everyone to sit down and watch me for a moment. When I hit this drum, I am going to change shapes, and I will freeze in that new shape just like a statue." Hit the drum and freeze in a shape, hit the drum again and jump and freeze in a new shape. Stay frozen for a dramatic length of time. Do not even move your eyes. Since you have a drum in your hand, freezing in a twisted shape may be easiest for effect. Do about four freezes. "OK, now I want you to try this. Find a starting shape and ... freeze!" Say "freeze!" and hit the drum several times. Give space between each freeze for the child to feel the stillness. You can make suggestions—that the shapes be high, low, tough, pretty.
    "Now I want you to walk while I beat the drum, and freeze when I say 'freeze!' Are you ready? Take your first shape and

freeze! OK, here we go. Walk, walk, walk, walk, walk, walk." Hit the drum each time you say "walk." After about 10 beats, say "freeze!" "Good. Beautiful shapes! Let's go again." Repeat about 10 times, occasionally specifying the quality of the shapes.

Extensions: Refer to floor crossings (p. 60) for ideas on locomotion. Shape suggestions: high, middle, low, twisted, straight, curvy, monsterlike, birdlike, snakelike, big, little, babylike.

Once the activity is established, you can count to 10 instead of beating the drum.

Develop the activity in the usual way, and then ask the children to freeze connected to someone else. Usually the connection will be hands and arms reaching and touching another. Encourage other kinds of connections with body parts such as feet, hips, and arms; or specify connecting with no hands. Sculptures that children create are very interesting. Be certain to point them out to your class.

Notes: Freeze! is one of the richest activities in this book. With *Freeze!* you can use all the elements of movement. Children are challenged and absorbed by this activity. Be certain to pick up ideas for what to do by watching the children. They come up with wonderful shapes and amazing ways to move from space to space. Recognize what they are doing by having other children try the shape or movement.

"Now I'm Walking"

Objectives: To be able to move vigorously and then be still.

Consideration: This activity is most appropriate for four-year-old children.

Directions: "I would like everyone to come over here and sit down. I want you to watch me. Are you ready?"

"Now I'm Big." Each child has chosen a different way to move "big."

C   F   D   C   D   C   D   C
Now I'm walk - ing, walk - ing, walk - ing.
Follow the directions.

C   F   D   C   D   E   F
Now I'm walk - ing. Now I'm still.

Be very still and do not move your eyes for a dramatic length of time. Repeat your example without the children.

"Are you ready to try it now? You need to be able to be very still. I don't want to be able to see a hair move." Concentrate on stillness until the concept of how to be motionless is firmly embedded in the children. Progress to running and then to any of the locomotions in floor crossings (p. 60) and to in-place movements (p. 63).

Notes: Look carefully for ideas from the children. They are always trying new things. When you ask them to walk, someone may start moving sideways. Use that as the next direction.

In *Freeze!* there is emphasis on making shapes. In this exercise there is emphasis on freezing in the middle of a walk or run. This creates a very interesting, special kind of shape, a pedestrian shape. There is a frozen-in-time quality to this activity.

Movement and body awareness

The activities in this section are less vigorous than those for warming up. At times, attention is focused upon the individual child's movements. By watching others move, we learn more about our own movement. We acquire ideas for movement and we develop a stronger notion of what our own bodies might look like if we were to do a similar activity. Because young children are moving toward abstract thinking, they are in the learning stages of being able to see their bodies as others might see them. We talk of *shape* in movement classes but only older children are able to understand clearly what we mean. Much of what we do in movement is to educate children about the visual shape their bodies make as they stop in space or as they move in space. In strength and groundedness activities (p. 71) and in trust and sensitivity activities (p. 83) we educate children about the inner energies of the body and about the body's effect upon others.

Because children are working in front of others in some of these exercises, the teacher needs to be very sensitive to the child's pride. It is wise to alternate easier activities with more difficult ones. If you suspect that children vary from your directions because they fear they cannot do the specified movement, let it go and work with the child privately, later, if possible. Often, a new movement in which the others can benefit by trying emerges in such a situation. If so, you can turn the child's feelings of inadequacy into a feeling of pride at having contributed new material to the class. For example, if you have asked children to hop individually across the floor on one foot, and one child jumps across on two feet, you can say, "That's a good idea too. Let's all try Jonathan's way this time."

In this section, specific objectives are provided with each activity. General objectives for movement and body awareness activities include these: to acquire an understanding of *shape*, to explore new movements, to recognize different body parts and to explore their function, to solve problems.

Floor Crossings

Objectives: To explore various locomotions. To learn names of various locomotions. To move in front of others with ease.

Considerations: This activity works well with younger children using the simpler kinds of locomotion. Determine ahead of time where the crossings will be in the room and how to define where children sit and wait for their turns on each side of the crossing space. The crossing space should be about 15 feet long. Use tape on the floor, carpet squares, a wall, or anything you think of to define the place where children should wait on each side. Children must always be sitting between turns. Determine also whether there is room for all the children to cross at once in a more controlled locomotion like crawling, or if you need to divide the group in half.

Directions: "Everyone come over to this side of the room. Please sit down behind this line. Now I want you to lie down on your belly like this. We're all going to wriggle across the room like a bunch of lizards or snakes on our bellies. Here we go. That was great. Now everyone needs to stay behind this line over here. I'm going over to the other side of the room, and when I call your name, I want you to crawl over to me any way you want—fast, slow—you decide. OK. Mark, you come first." As the children arrive, pat the floor where you want them to sit. Continue using different kinds of locomotor activities from the list which follows.

Extensions: Children who are waiting can clap hands or repeat a word to mark the beat and support the crosser(s).

You can use the same format to do activities in Part IV for one child and one adult working together. Seat the children on one side of the room and call them one by one to be balanced on your feet, for example. They then go to the other side of the room to wait for the next activity.

Notes: Begin the session on the floor because this gives a more secure feeling to the children in this new activity. Alternate large group crossings with individual or pair crossings. If things are moving too slowly and the children are becoming restless, have the children come in pairs or trios. The reasons for the individual crossings are that the child has a maximum amount of space and does not need to worry about collisions, and that the teacher can focus more clearly on what each child is doing. Additionally, some children bloom with this opportunity for individual recognition. The group crossings prevent restlessness from sitting and waiting for a turn. They also provide an opportunity for children to learn to move without collision.

It is your job as teacher to make appropriate comments as children are crossing the floor. You should make a remark about each child's action. Comment on a special feature of what they are doing so that the children can come to understand the infinite variety available in every movement. Ask the children to watch for differences in movement. For example, if children are doing long body rolls across the floor, ask the watching children if a particular roller has the arms above the head or by the side of the body. Watch the following rollers and repeat the question. Children will begin making a conscious choice about where they put their arms. If a child does something interesting, have the whole group give it a try.

Suggestions for floor crossings

These are arranged in approximate order of difficulty within each type. Those activities with an asterisk may be used for group crossings. However, be sure to use them as individual crossings also.

Low level

long body roll
*belly crawl
*moving forward, sitting
*moving backward, sitting
*back on ground, scooting
*hip walking
*seal walk (using arms, legs dragging)
sitting up roll (palms, hips, and legs on the floor)
curled-up roll

Middle level

*crawling
*knee walk
*squatting walk
*frog jumps
*four-legged walk—belly down
*walk on knees and elbows
*walk holding onto ankles
semicartwheels
four-legged walk—belly up

High level

*walk
run
*tip-toe walk
*giant steps
*pogo jumps
run through held-up large scarf
run and hit drum or tambourine with one hand
run and hit drum or tambourine with two hands
*march/high-knee walk
*stomp
*straight-leg walk
*walk on heels
*shuffle (without lifting feet from ground)
*slide walk (without lifting feet from ground)
kicking walk
*cross-over steps—one foot swings out and around in front of other
hop
*gallop
turn
punch air with fists as you walk
run and jump to hit drum
*lunge
leap
run and jump
run and leap
run and freeze in a shape
run and fall down and roll
swinging arm broad jump
*skip
run and slide

Other floor-crossing suggestions

Most of these can be done as a group crossing. However, because they invite children to show their own special inventions, be certain to use them as individual or pair crossings too. These are not arranged in order of difficulty. Emotional qualities are more difficult for children to portray than motional qualities.

monster	all jiggly
robot	all smooth
king/queen	all twisty
baby	how slow
mommy/daddy	how fast
emotions (mad, sad, happy)	the hardest way to go
being tall	the easiest way to go
being big	backward
being small	sideways
on the ground	very strong
in your middle level	very weak
as high as you can go	your favorite way
as various animals	

In-Place Movement

Objective: To explore new movements.

Directions: "I would like all of you to find your own space on the floor. Kneel down like I am and stretch your arms out. Now turn your body slowly and see if your fingers touch anyone as you move. If your fingers touch someone, you need to move yourself so that you have more room. This is called finding your own space—a place where you can move without touching anyone. Now I want all of you to sit down and to slap the floor with the soles of your feet like I am. OK, now let's rub our bodies all over with our hands. Do your arms, your legs, your feet, your chest, and your stomach. Can you rub your back? Don't forget your head and face. Now let's lie on our backs and pretend we're riding a bicycle with our legs. Great." Continue with other activities from the list which follows.

Extension: Divide group in half and have one group watch the other group.

"Using your hands and your feet, balance on three points."

Suggestions for in-place movements

This is by no means a complete list. Many of the sitting down movements can be done standing up. None of the sitting down movements are difficult so they are listed randomly. Other in-place movements are listed in the approximate order of difficulty.

Sitting down movements

slap floor with soles of feet	tickle body parts
pat body parts	shake body parts
scratch body parts	stretch all over
rub body parts	jiggle all over

clap feet

clap body parts together (elbow/knee, foot/hand, foot/head)

clap hands over head, behind back, under legs

blink eyes

open and shut mouth, chew

open and close leg, arm; together, separately

flap wings

spin on buttocks, using hands

spin on buttocks, using hands, and then without hands

Other in-place movements

jump in place

stomp feet

run in place

turn in place

lie on back, curl into a ball, and roll

make a bridge, belly down

lie on back and ride a bicycle

collapse to the ground

in crawl position, make back go up and down like a cat's

balance on one foot, hold the other foot

spin on stomach

swing arms together up to one side, then to the other; let

body go with the movement

sway back and forth on hands and feet

balance on one knee

supporting yourself on straight arms, be a kicking, bucking horse

make a bridge, belly up

jump into the air, turn around, and come down

balance on two arms and one knee, then move

roll backward over your shoulder

The Drum Beat Game

Objectives: To respond instantly to a cue. To experiment with different movements.

Considerations: A drum is needed for this activity, which works well with younger children.

Directions: "Each of you needs to find your own space in the room. We are going to play a game. When I hit the drum, I want you to fall on the ground. Are you ready?" Drum beat. "Great. You really went down fast. Let's do it again. I want to see you collapse to the floor like you've been hit when you hear the drum." Wait a moment. Sound another drum beat. "OK. Now this time when you hear the drum beat, I want you to run and touch the wall. Ready?" Drum beat. "This time I want you to touch another wall. Ready?" Drum beat. "Everyone back into the center of the room, because this time I want you to jump into the air. Do you have your own space? Remember, you're going to jump in the air when you hear the drum beat. Are you ready?" Drum beat. "Let's do that one again. Up in the air. Ready?" Drum beat. "This time I want you to fall to the ground again. Are you ready?" Drum beat.

Extensions: For older children, the movements can be more complex and/or in a series: up in the air, down to the ground, and backward to a wall.

Divide the group in half so one half can watch the other.

Other suggestions: punch the air, be a bucking horse, do a somersault, turn around, make a face, make a shape, start jiggling all over, turn into a bird.

Notes: With a continuing action, such as being a bucking horse, it will be necessary to say "Freeze!" or "Everybody sit down" to prepare the children for your next activity.

Knees

Objectives: To clearly identify the knees. To understand their movement.

Considerations: You can do this activity as part of your beginning circle activities. The younger children can take part for the first half of this activity.

Directions: "Where are your knees? Let's give them a rub to say hello. Now let's tap them. That feels different, doesn't it? Maybe your knees would like to say hello to each other. Hello, knee, hello, knee. Your elbows can say hello to your knees too. Hello, knees, hello, knees. Can anything else say hello to your knees? Oh, your head can. And your foot. Hello, hello, hello. Let's make our knees straight and bend them up again. Let's do that again. Straighten and bend. Straighten and bend. Can you walk on your knees? Great. Can you walk on just your knees, no feet touching the floor. That's harder, isn't it? Are your knees beginning to hurt? Well they're not really made for walking on. They're really made for straightening and bending. Let's sit down and do that again. Maisha, come over here. I want to see you jump as high as you can. Good. Now I want everyone to watch Maisha's knees as she jumps. Can you see how they bend and then straighten? Maisha, do it one more time for us, so that we can really see. OK, who else would like to show us how high you can jump so that we can watch your knees bend and straighten? OK, Jules, Mary, and Andrew you show us next." Continue until all of the children who choose to do so have shown their highest jumps.

Extensions: This activity in part can focus on other body joints such as elbows, wrists, or ankles to help children clearly identify the parts.

The Tunnel

Objective: To help create a special space for others.

Directions: "I would like everyone to sit down. When I call your name, come here and put your body like this." Put your body in a crawling position. "Angela, you come first. OK, Marius you're next. You go right next to Angela." Continue until all of the children are in a line, shoulder to shoulder. "Each one of you is going to get to crawl through this long, dark tunnel that your bodies make. It is very important that you not move and that you take good care of the people going through. Angela, you're first. That's right, you get to crawl under all those bodies right through to the other end. OK, Angela, now you need to help make the tunnel here at this end. And it's Marius' turn." Continue until all of the children have had a chance to go through the tunnel.

Extensions: Use the floor crossings format and have the children work in couples. One person makes a tunnel for the other and then they reverse roles.

Encourage different kinds of tunnels: bellies up, bellies down, through the arms, through an arm and a leg, two people making a tunnel for another. The teacher can make the tunnels or the teacher can crawl through the tunnels.

Notes: Tunnels can be made in an infinite variety of ways. Children love them. They love to make them for each other. Experiment with different ways.

Pushing Feet

Objective: To coordinate foot and leg pressure with another person's foot and leg pressure.

Consideration: This activity is fairly brief.

Directions: "I would like everyone to sit down on the floor right where you are and to watch. Nicole and Jasmine, I want you to lie down on your backs and to put your feet together. Doesn't that feel nice? OK. Now you may need to scoot closer together or farther apart, but I want you to push your feet against each other's and to see what sorts of designs you can make. Great. Look how high they can get their feet. It takes a lot of coordination to keep your feet together like this. Can you ride a bicycle together?

That is really hard, but see if you can do that. Let's everyone try it."
Put the children into pairs. Suggest that they scoot closer together so that there is an even foot pressure or farther apart if they
look too awkward.

Props

Objectives: To experience free movement. To experiment with
new movements. To see the effect of movement upon an inani-
mate object. To feel speed. To avoid collisions.

Considerations: This should be the last activity of the session
before a relaxation because of the distractibility of the materials.
One of these props should be provided for each child: balloons,
crepe paper streamers, scarves, or pieces of fabric (rectangles six
inches by four feet). A record and a phonograph are useful.
Choose music you enjoy dancing to. Ballet music, such as
Tchaikovsky's "Nutcracker Suite," is wonderful. Michael Olatunji's *Drums of Passion and More Drums of Passion* (Columbia
Record #CG33654) and Leonard Bernstein's "West Side Story"
invite dancing. However, if rock and roll or the samba inspire you,
then certainly use your favorite. This works well with younger
children. A larger space is good.

Directions: "Everyone come over here and sit down with me.
Today we have something very special. I have a long piece of
crepe paper for each one of you. I want you to take this piece of
crepe paper and I want to see you make it fly. I even have some
special flying music for you. When you have your crepe paper,
take off, and let's see it fly."

Extensions: Suggest, while the children are working, that they
make the streamer fly high or low or in the middle, that they make
it jerky, and then smooth. Can they run backwards and make it
fly? Can they make it go high and low?

At the end of the time, bring the children to one side of the room and have them do floor crossings, one at a time, doing their favorite things with the crepe paper.

Notes: Pieces of fabric and scarves have properties similar to the streamers. Wider pieces of fabric can be held to the shoulders like a cape and be made to fly.

Balloons are a challenge to keep in the air. Older children can try to keep a balloon up without using their hands.

Mirroring

Objective: To reproduce approximately the motions of the leader.

Consideration: This activity is appropriate for older children.

Directions: "I would like everyone to sit along this line." Sit on the ground facing the line of children. "Now I would like you to do exactly what I do. You need to really concentrate in order to do this." Slowly move one arm only. When you arrive at a stopping point with that arm, move the other arm. It is important that only one body part at one time be moving or that if two body parts are moving, that they be moving in unison. Try to make your movements predictable, so that the followers do not get lost. Use pedestrian movements such as eating or putting your hand on your hip. Tricking the followers is not appropriate. Head movements are possible but the eyes must return to a forward position in order to see the leader. Face movements, such as chewing, blinking, or opening your mouth work well.

When the group has gained confidence in a sitting position, you can stand. Move in place at first, and then to the sides. Moving forward and backward is complicated because the impluse is to step backward when the leader steps forward. You can do rapid movements like patting, rubbing, or scratching to break the slow movement. Because concentration is great, stop before the children become restless. You can talk to the children as you work to create a small drama, or you can be silent.

Extensions: Children should have opportunities to try leading, but leading is difficult. Leaders need to be able to project what effect their actions will have upon the followers. There is a great sense of power in leading.

Note: The children are seated in a line so that they do not have easy eye contact with one another.

Strength and groundedness

The ground assumes an extraordinarily important role for the child who is learning to move. It is stable and dependable. It does not move. It is always there. Though the surface may vary, the quality of solidness does not.

Our strength comes from the ground. If people have a firm connection with the ground, they can push, pull, lift, and support weight, in addition to punching and other forms of striking out. If people have a firm connection with the ground, they cannot be moved easily.

Understanding and supporting our connection with the ground is a very important principle of movement education. Strength gives people a very basic sense of power. Children who are able to focus their strength, and whose strength is recognized by others, are confident children.

Some girls do not feel they have permission to be physically strong. They have instead developed strength in communication skills or in small motor activities but they have never explored being physically strong. A strong girl is not valued by many people in our culture. At three and four, children are exploring what it is to be male and what it is to be female. Categories perceived by children are sometimes very rigid, particularly around the age of five. "Girls don't fight" or "Boys don't play with dolls" become rigid rules. Their rigidity is based upon observation of our world as it is and the need children have to define who they are and what behavior is appropriate. The child who deviates from the expectations of the adults and children around her or him is truly expressing a very strong personal need.

For boys, developing strength is vitally important. A strong man is looked up to in our society. All of the superhero fantasies are based on strength. Teachers often have mixed feelings about boys' expressions of strength. Where and when is it appropriate? Should we encourage it? What about the self-image of the boy who does not feel strong?

In recent years, we have begun to recognize the ways in which we have limited our children by supporting traditional roles. We may now look for nurturing males and strong females to provide models for our children. We read stories in which it is all right for boys to play with dolls and for girls to do carpentry. We talk a lot about how girls can be doctors and truck drivers and about how boys can be nurses and teachers; and this talk is important. However, in addition to models and materials and talk, we speak to the children through our curriculum and through our actions about what we value.

If supporting strength becomes a part of the curriculum, both boys and girls benefit. To the strong girls and boys the teacher is saying, "I value your competence in this area. I, too, think being strong is very important, and I will provide for you nonviolent ways of showing your strength." Violence and strength are two different things. This difference should be discussed along with the responsibilities that go with being strong.

To the less strong girls and boys the teacher is saying, "I think being strong is important for everyone. I will help you to feel your strength and to know that you, too, are strong."

In some of these activities, one child is asked to place total body weight upon another. Children may be hesitant to do this with very heavy peers. Unless the child is extremely heavy, the weight can be absorbed easily. The weight should be distributed evenly over the supporter's body. The weight should feel good to the supporter. Heavy children should *never* be excluded from activities because of their weight. Do not do the activity if you feel the weight cannot be handled.

The results of doing activities built around strength and groundedness are gratifying. Children are involved and challenged by them. A special relationship of mutual respect develops among the participants. I believe that a sense of trust develops between the teacher and students that overflows to other curriculum areas.

Many of these activities are for partners. Sometimes it is possible to ask the children to choose their own partner. Often it is necessary to assign partners so that children of approximately the same weight are together, or so that one person is not consistently left out.

The partner activities are set up so that one set of partners at a time is working. This is so that the teacher can really focus on that couple to make certain they understand and follow the directions. Often the teacher will need to hand-guide the first couple. She or he should choose this couple carefully. They should be children who are apt to understand quickly what is wanted. Once the children have seen the activity done properly, they need less guidance.

Because most of the children are onlookers, it is important that there be a vigorous total group activity prior to a couple activity. Couple activities can be one of a sequence of floor-crossing activities also, since the setup is similar.

The teacher should comment to the onlookers while the couple is working. The comments should be positive and should reflect an admiration for strength and for caring. The comments should also be about the different ways each person approaches the problem. Comments about the placement of different body parts sensitize the children to the function of each part in a given activity. The performing couple will take in the teacher's comments to the onlookers, usually without losing concentration, and the comments help to involve the onlookers in the action.

Specific objectives are given with each activity. General objectives for strength-and-groundedness activities are to feel a personal strength, to learn to focus strength, to learn to use strength constructively, and to understand that the ground is the source of strength.

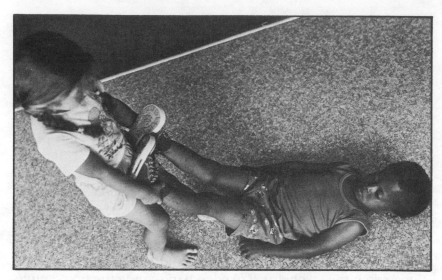

Pulling demonstrates strength. Being pulled demonstrates trust. The children's roles will be reversed when she reaches the end of her path.

Pulling a Partner

Objectives: To feel strength through moving another body. To relax when another person is pulling you.

Considerations: This activity works well with younger children. A smooth floor is required. The floor-crossings setup is used (p. 60).

Directions: "I would like everyone over on this side of the room with me. Today, we are going to do something special. I am carefully going to give each of you a very special ride across the room. Who would like to be first? Jessica. You need to lie down on your back. Now I am going to pick up your legs by the ankles and very carefully pull you across the room. There. Did you like that?" Pull each of the children in turn, but only if they agree. "OK. Now who feels that you could pull someone across the floor? Olivia and Corey, let's have you two first. Olivia, you lie down. Corey, pick up Olivia's ankles. That's right. Now be very careful, and let me see you pull Olivia across the room. Beautiful. Can you see how careful Corey is being? And Olivia is very relaxed. She really trusts Corey. That's beautiful. Now put her feet down on the floor very gently. Good. Now you wait on this side of the room and in just a minute, Olivia can pull Corey." Continue with the other children.

Extensions: Children can be pulled fast or slow and in curvy paths or in straight lines.

See if two children on each leg can pull you.

Rolling a Partner

Objectives: To feel strength through moving another body. To know where to push to make a body roll. To relax and let another person roll you.

Considerations: With younger children, the adult can do all of the manipulation. The floor-crossings setup is used (p. 60).

Directions: "I would like everyone over on this side of the room with me. Now I'm going to go over to the other side of the room, and when I call your name, I want you to begin rolling across the floor to me. Gabrielle." Call each of the children's names in turn. "OK. Now this time each person is going to roll across the floor, but that person isn't going to do any of the work. Ryan and Maisha, you come first, and I'll show you what to do. Ryan, you lie down on the floor all stretched out with your arms over your head. Now I want you to really relax. Just like you're going to take a nap. I don't want you to do anything. Maisha is going to do all of the work. Maisha, I want you to roll Ryan carefully across the floor. I want everyone to watch how Maisha does this. Ryan, you don't do anything. Maisha is strong, and she's doing all the work."

Continue with the other children. They should all return across the floor with the person who was rolled becoming the person who rolls the other. As much as possible, keep partners together to create a reciprocal arrangement.

Extension: Let four children roll you.

Notes: The greatest difficulty is usually for the one being rolled to resist helping out. It is important that the child be a dead weight as much as possible.

Many children seem to know intuitively that they need to push or pull in the hip area.

Pushing Fronts

Objectives: To feel strength. To feel the ground as the source of that strength.

Considerations: This activity can be done as a part of floor crossings since it involves the same setup (see p. 60).

Directions: "Everyone come over here with me to this side of the room and sit down. Today, I want to do something very special. I want to feel how strong each one of you is. Monica, why don't you be first? Come here with me." Go to the center of the room where there is more space. "I'm going to kneel down but, Monica, I want you to stay standing. I'm kneeling just because I'm so tall, and I want to be more Monica's height. OK now. Monica, I want you to push against my hands really hard. Don't try to push me over. I just want to feel how strong you are. Good. That's very good. You are very strong. I can really feel how strong you are. Can you see how Monica is pushing against the floor with her legs and feet? That is the reason she is so strong. She knows how to put her body right. Thank you, Monica. Now please sit on the other side of the room and watch while I work with Victor.

Extensions: If the children have done this with you successfully, try putting them in couples. Work with one couple at a time and emphasize that they are to balance their strength. They are not to try to push each other over.

Rocks

Objectives: To feel a personal focus of energy and strength. To be able to focus energy where it is needed in response to a given pressure. To feel a connection with the ground.

Considerations: This can be an ending activity, used in the middle of the session, or added as part of a fantasy. This activity should be introduced to three-year-olds; they will understand it more clearly at four.

Directions: "I would like each of you to find your own place on the floor, and I want you to kneel down like this." Kneel into a tight ball with your head down. "You are rocks. You are very strong rocks. You are so heavy on the ground. You have been sitting here for years and years. It is as though you have roots that grow way deep down into the earth. You are solid and you are strong. Now I am very strong, and I am going to come around and try to push each one of these rocks over. OK. Here is my first rock. It is a beautiful green and red striped rock. It looks pretty tough. Let me see if I can push it over." Grunt and groan as you push. Use a firm, whole-hand pressure; use both hands sometimes. Your first child should be someone you think will probably be fairly solid. If the child does not resist your pressure, put one hand on the other side of the body so that you are helping the child to resist the pressure. Work on one place until you get resistance, and then move to another part of the body. If you get resistance, push or pull the child as hard as you can without pushing her or him over. Never push the child over. The child needs to really feel that you are strong and that you are really testing her or his strength. Places to focus on include hips, rib cage, and shoulders. However, you can try other parts more gently. Push and pull. Try pushing with your shoulder and arm or your hips as well as your hands.

Extensions: If the children have done this with you successfully, try putting them in couples. Work with one couple at a time, and emphasize that pushers need to use their muscles, but that they are not to push the other person over. They are to balance their strength against their partner's. Children readily understand this.

Straddle one child's body facing the head. Pick up the child a few inches from the floor with your hands around the ribs toward the hips. Tell the children that you want to see how hard the rocks are. Will the rocks uncurl when you pick them, or will they stay all tight and hard? You want the children to stay curled up. It is very difficult for some children.

Notes: Though you are speaking in fantasy terms here, if someone begins to come apart, be clear. "No. I don't want to be able to push you over. You must put your strength and energy where I am pressing so that I can't push you over. Now I want to see you really work. I know that you are strong and that you can do it." Be very serious and intense. Children will then work to try to center their energy. The younger children are just developing a sense of how to focus this energy and how to resist you, but most four-year-olds can do it and feel very challenged.

Turn Me Not

Objectives: To feel a personal centeredness and strength. To focus energy where it is needed in response to a given pressure. To feel a connection with the ground.

Considerations: This can be an ending activity, used in the mid-

Children feel enormous power when they can resist an adult's efforts to move them.

dle of the session, or added as part of a fantasy. This activity should be introduced to three-year-olds; they will understand it more clearly at four.

Directions: This activity is very similar to *Rocks*. Please refer to the directions, extensions, and notes for that activity, in addition to the directions below (p. 77).

"I would like each of you to find your own space. Lie down with your belly on the floor. Now I want you to feel how very strong you are. You are really attached to the floor. You have roots growing from your body down into the ground. I am going to come along, and I am going to try to turn you over. I don't want you to let me, but I am going to really try." Follow the general directions under *Rocks*. Concentrate on the torso though the entire body is extended. Try the arms and hands and legs and feet also, but the torso is of greatest importance. This activity is not easy for children. Often you have to talk them into concentrating their energy where you are pulling. "Feel where my hands are. Now I want you to really concentrate. Work. Feel my hands. Don't let them pull you." Relax your pull, and then try again, relax it, talk some more, and then try again. There is a great feeling of success when the child succeeds. The child knows it and you know it.

Staying Together

Objectives: To feel a personal centeredness and strength. To focus energy where it is needed in response to a given pressure.

Considerations: This can be an ending activity, used in the middle of the session, or added as part of a fantasy. This activity should be introduced to three-year-olds; they will understand it more clearly at four.

Directions: This activity is very similar to *Rocks.* Please refer to the directions, extensions, and notes for that activity, in addition to directions below (p. 77).

"I would like each of you to find your own space on the floor. Lie on your side, all curled up in a tight, little ball like this." Demonstrate. "Now I am going to come around, and I am going to try to pull these balls apart. I don't want you to let me. You are strong. I am really going to try to pull these balls apart, but you balls need to be stronger than I am. Are you ready?"

Pushing Backs

Objective: To balance one person's strength against another's.

Considerations: This activity is appropriate for older children. A smooth floor is required.

Directions: "Because our floor is so slippery, everyone needs to be in bare feet for this. I want you to come over and sit with me on this side of the room. Now you need to watch very closely what is going to happen. Everyone will have a chance to try this out, but I want you two to sit down here." Put the pair in a clear space where the others can see clearly. "I want you to sit with your backs together. Now listen while I tell you what to do. I want each of you to push against the back of the other, but I want you to take care of the other person. Don't push each other over. Ready? Push. Can you see how they're using their feet on the floor to push? And Jamal is even using his hands. They are pushing hard, but they are being careful to not push the other person over. OK. Now, Jamal, I want you to relax. Don't push at all. Just relax. Jennifer, I want you to give Jamal a little ride. Push against his back again and make him move—give him a ride. Jamal, you're not allowed to help her. Jennifer is really strong. She can push you. Great. Now, Jamal, you need to give Jennifer a push back to where you started. Jennifer, now you need to be the relaxed one. Let Jamal give *you* a ride. Good work. Did you see how strong these two people are? They have good strong legs and they pushed each other clear across the floor. You two need to come sit back down over here so you can watch the next two partners. Now, let's see who's next. I'm trying to put people together who weigh about the same."

Rides

Objectives: To feel strength when moving another body. To relax when another person is caring for you.

Considerations: This activity is appropriate for older children. The floor-crossings setup is used (p. 60).

Trusting the person who is supporting you is difficult. It is as important in this activity as being strong enough to support.

Directions: "I would like everyone over here with me. Today we're going to try something new. George and Sheila, would you like to be the first to do this? Good. George, curl up on the floor like a rock, OK? Now, Sheila, I want you to lie down on George's back so that your tummy is on his back. Beautiful. Do you feel solid and relaxed? You may need to move a little toward George's head. I don't want you to slip off. How does that feel, George? Good. OK. Now, George, I want you to get up so that you can crawl. Can you do that? Beautiful. You only need to go a little way. That's fine. OK. Now lower yourself back down to the floor. Don't move yet, Sheila. OK. Now, George, can you roll over to the side so that Sheila can roll off? That is just beautiful. Did everyone see that? What a beautiful roll you both did. All right, in just a minute Sheila will carry George back, but let's give another couple a turn."

Extensions: When the couple crawls, the one on top can help also, and then they look like a marvelous eight-legged, two-headed creature.

The child on top can lie back to back.

Growing

Objective: To feel a strong connection with the ground.

Consideration: This activity is appropriate for older children.

Directions: "Curl up on the ground like a little ball. Put your hands on the ground and rock back and forth, back and forth, back and forth. The ground is so firm and solid. It is right there for you. Now you can begin crawling all around. Crawl in and out of all the other crawlers. Let's crawl really fast. And now let's crawl really slow. Now I want you to get bigger. I want you to move on your arms and hands and feet like a four-legged animal. Your arm-legs are just as strong as your leg-legs. See if you can leap up and land in a crouch just like a monkey. Leap up and crouch. Leap up and crouch. Now you are growing taller. You are a person who can run lightly and carefully around all these other people. You can jump into the air and land so lightly. You can leap into the air and turn around and come back down. You can run and leap and run again. You are so light, like a bird. This time you can leap into the air and come all the way down to the ground where you began. Can you feel the ground under you? It holds you up, and it takes care of you. Rest."

Trust and sensitivity

Trust in others is the basis of growth. In order for a teacher to facilitate growth, that teacher must have acquired the trust of the students. This trust is built through the words we say and the tone of voice we use, through observations of us by the children, through the ways we touch the children, through the confidence of the parents in the teachers. Children base their judgments of others upon innumerable, small factors just as adults do.

Sensitivity to the feelings of others and to our personal effect upon others is a long educational process. This learning is particularly intense during the years of three and four. Children are still developing the ability to empathize with others. Children often look puzzled when you tell them that they stepped on someone's hand or that it hurts when they jump on your back. Developmentally, children are beginning to understand that other people hurt and have feelings in the same way that they do. It is our job as teachers to assist children in acquiring this understanding.

Sensitivity builds trust. The child can think, "I can trust you because you have been sensitive to my needs," and then, "You can trust me because I have been sensitive to your needs."

Trust and sensitivity activities should be presented after a group has been together for awhile. Children need to have time to know one another casually. These activities are not overwhelming, but they have more meaning for a group who knows one another well. The children learn to view each other in new kinds of ways through these activities. For example, David is always the superhero. Lifting David up and transporting him to another place transforms David into a person dependent upon others.

These activities are wonderful to bring into fantasies (p. 92). For example, if someone is blinded by the volcano's eruption, that person will need to be led home through all the fallen rocks by a sighted person.

Some activities were not included because they are difficult to fit into a group format but these are ideas you might like to find space for one day.

- Some younger children love to roll up in sheets. It seems somewhat like swaddling. It does not bother them at all or cause panic if their faces are covered.

- Children really like to jump over each other which could be considered the ultimate trusting situation. Mistakes are never serious, and they are infrequent. I let children jump over me. First

I lie still and then I roll slowly.

- See if an older child can walk to you with eyes closed. At first, make the distance short, and then see if you can increase it. Receive the child with firm, ready hands.
- When children crawl across the floor, see if they can do it with closed eyes.
- Ask a child if she or he would like to run with closed eyes, holding onto your hand. Running is particularly disorienting because both feet are off the ground at the same time.

Specific objectives are given with each activity. General objectives for trust and sensitivity activities are to learn to trust your body to another and to learn to care for another.

The Cradle

Objective: To care for another.

Consideration: This works well with younger children.

Directions: "Everyone come over here with me. Let's sit down. Now, I would like to really take care of someone. Would someone here really like me to take care of you? Marcos. Good. Now I need two people to help me take care of Marcos. Elizabeth and Jonah. OK. Now, Elizabeth and Jonah, you and I need to figure out how to make a cradle for Marcos. Can you scoot over next to me and let's see what we can do." The cradle can be formed in any way that works for the three of you. More children can be involved if you would like. "Marcos, can you very gently put yourself into this cradle? Good. Now, Marcos, see if you can close your eyes and let us rock you just as though you were a little baby. Of course you're not, but we'll just pretend. Elizabeth and Jonah, let's rock Marcos back and forth and sing to him. Do you know 'Rock-A-Bye Baby?' "

Notes: If there is any laughing or teasing, it needs to be stopped quickly. The younger the group the less likelihood of its occurrence. If it is an older group, arrange the activity so that the child being rocked does not have eye contact with the onlookers.

Lazy Sways

Objective: To develop trust.

Considerations: This is a good ending activity. It works well with younger children.

Directions: "Each of you needs to find your own space on the floor. Lie down on your back and feel how nice and solid the floor feels under your back. Now I am going to come around and do something special with each one of you." Go to the first child, stand straddling Jonathan, facing his head. Pick up his arms at the wrist; slowly and gently lift the upper half of his body. The child's head should drop back, but very likely will not. Ask the child to let his head drop back. Tell him that you will take care of him. If he is very young and does not understand your words, see if you can put both wrists in one of your hands, and then put your other hand under his head assuming the weight of the head. Then lower the head in your hand. Releasing the head is important because if the child is holding it up, his body is rigid. It is also a signal of how much he trusts the situation. Once the head is dropped back, gently and slowly sway the child's torso from side to side. You can also alternately pull the arms toward you slowly, so that the left and the right sides of the torso alternately raise and lower. Occasionally a child will spontaneously close her or his eyes! "Now I am going to very gently lower you back to the ground." Sometimes the head gets caught with the crown on the floor and will not slide so the back of the head is on the floor. Again put both wrists in one hand and lean down with your other hand to help the head slide to the back.

Extension: Older children can do this to each other, but they need to be closely supervised.

Rolling Over

Objectives: To learn how to move over other people's bodies without hurting them. To cooperate with each other in order to provide a special experience for one.

Directions: "Everyone come over to this side of the room with me." Everyone needs to start at one end of the room because the group gradually moves to the other end of the room. "I want you to all lie down on the floor on your bellies, shoulder to shoulder, and very close together. Julie, you lie down first, and then Corey, and .... Now Julie is closest to the wall so she will begin. Julie, you are going to roll over this line of bodies. You need to be careful of people and you need to roll fairly quickly." Watch for knees and elbows. It hurts to have these rolled over. Also watch to make sure the rolling child does not press down with her knees or elbows or hands upon the other children's bodies. The children do not understand if you tell them—only through experience and your constant reminders will they come to be aware of how to roll over others with minimum discomfort. The children often roll crookedly, so you need to help them stay on the torsos. "Great, Julie. Now you lie down on this end, and Corey you're the next to roll. Be gentle getting on. Here he comes." Continue until the entire line has rolled and Julie is once again at the beginning.

Notes: Heavy children are sometimes hesitant and others may tease, if the children are older. It is important that these children roll also. Because the roller moves quickly, it is quite a cushioned roll, and the pressure is never on one place for more than a second.

Resting

Objectives: To feel the weight of another person. To put your weight gently on another person. To feel the quiet space of two people resting together.

Consideration: This activity is a good ending activity.

Directions: "You each need to find your own space on the floor. Now I would like you to curl up tightly like a strong, hard rock. You may watch while I go around and talk to people, but I don't want you to move. Just rest right where you are." Put couples together as you move around the floor. Speak in a low voice to set the mood of quiet. "Janice and Denis, I am going to put you two together. Janice, you stay where you are. Denis, I want you to very carefully lie down on Janice's back with your belly on her back, so that you are really comfortable and resting. Janice, you aren't going to go anywhere. You are to stay right where you are until I come back. Janice is a nice, comfortable, quiet bed, and Denis is taking a small rest on this nice bed." Continue, arranging the other pairs until they are all finished. When all of the couples have been arranged, say, "I want you to feel the silence and the closeness, and then I will come around and help you to change positions." Allow there to be a few moments of silence, and then go back to Denis and Janice and have them reverse positions. Do the same with the other pairs in order. Provide a moment of silence at the end once again.

Extensions: The children can lie back to back.

The rock can be stretched out long on his tummy, and the rester can either lie lengthwise on his whole body or just place a part of her body on his.

The rock can determine his own way of being strong and supporting the weight.

Falling

Objectives: To trust the teacher to catch you. To make the body sufficiently rigid so that you fall without buckling.

Considerations: Some children have great difficulty doing this. This is a good ending activity.

Directions: "I would like to do something different today. You need to really be able to trust me to do this. You are going to fall onto my hands, and I am going to catch you. Who would like to be first? Keith." Keith stands in front of you. You need to kneel or stand firmly facing the child so that your open palms are at his chest. The distance between the child's chest and your palms should be short at the beginning of each child's experience. Increase the distance as you work with each child. When the child falls, accept the weight on your hands and let your hands move toward you a bit before you push the child upright. This acceptance movement makes the initial weight less, and gives you a momentum for moving the child back to an upright posture. It is very simple, and large five-year-olds are not difficult to handle. If the child cannot give you her or his weight, put one hand on the child's chest and the other on the back at the same point. Move the child's body forward until the weight is on the chest hand. Do this several times. In time the child will learn to trust you.

Rock-A-Bye Baby

Objectives: To support someone. To trust someome to take care of you.

Consideration: The floor-crossings setup is used (p. 60).

Directions: "Everyone come and sit with me on this side of the room. Today we are going to play a special game where you really need to take care of each other. Isaac and George, why don't you come first. George, you kneel down like this." Demonstrate a crawling posture. "Now, Isaac, I want you to very carefully lie on George's back. You can lie with your stomach down or up. I want you to feel very relaxed. George is your bed, and he's going to take good care of you. Now, George, I want you to gently rock back and forth. You need to take good care of Isaac. You are responsible for him. You want to rock back and forth very smoothly so that he can take a little rest. We're all going to sing a little song for you." Sing "Rock-A-Bye Baby." "Now, I'm glad you didn't let Isaac fall. He was really trusting you. But now, let's see how you can let him down very gently so he doesn't hurt himself."

Extension: Three children can line up shoulder to shoulder and then a fourth child lies on their backs.

Note: George should be able to devise his own way to put Isaac on the floor if he has had experience with *Rides* (p. 81).

Lifting Others

Objectives: To understand where body weight is located. To entrust yourself to others. To care for another. To learn that a group of people has great power.

Considerations: This activity is appropriate for older children. See the extensions for a modification that works well with younger children. A mat or a cluster of pillows is necessary if your floor is hard.

Directions: "Come sit down with me. Today we are going to do something which requires a great deal of strength. It also requires a lot of care. People will need to be very, very careful in this activity. We are going to see if we can pick someone up. Who would like to be lifted? Thelma. Good. Who is going to help lift? I think four people will be enough. Carlos, Martha, Eddy, and Olivia. Everyone else should watch to see if we can do this. Thelma, come and lie down on this mat. Now I am going to stand by Thelma's head and carry that, but how are we going to lift the rest of her body? Fine. Two people on each side. I think that looks good. Now let's kneel down by Thelma, and you put your hands on her very gently and very calmly, so that Thelma will know that she can trust you. Where do you think she is heaviest? That's right. This whole part of Thelma is called her torso, and if we lift her there, her arms and legs will just come along with the torso. Now put your hands where you think you should lift. But don't lift yet. That looks good. I will count to 3, and we will lift. 1, 2, 3, lift. Good. Now let's lower her head a little and lift her back up, down a little, and back up, down a little, and back up. And now the most important part. Very slowly and gently let's lower her to the floor together. Beautiful. How did that feel, Thelma?" Listen to her response. "Well, I think you were very brave. You really trusted these other people. I am very impressed. Also, you people really took care of Thelma. You really paid attention and worked together very well. You are strong in your muscle and you are strong on working together."

Extensions: The child can also be carried from one mat to another.

Younger children can be lifted in a sheet with an adult on either side of the sheet at the child's torso and children helping on the edges. The ride is the focus, rather than the strength involved in lifting, with the younger ones.

Notes: One of the main problems with this activity is that children do not have a long enough attention span to give each child who wants to be lifted a turn in one day. Each child needs to have the experience if one child does. One solution is to give two children per day a turn until all have been lifted.

Blind Walk

Objective: To trust another.

Considerations: Some children have great difficulty closing their eyes. Only those who really want to should do this. This activity is most appropriate for older children.

Directions: "Come sit down on the floor here with me. Today we are going to do something very, very special. Michael, would you like to try this out?" It is important to ask someone first who you think will think this is a terrific idea. "OK. Now I am going to take very good care of you. I will not let you bump into anything or hurt yourself in any way. We are just going to walk over to the window and back. You need to close your eyes. Are you ready?" Walk with Michael over to the window and back. Do not do anything fancy. Tell him where you are at every point. "Beautiful, Michael. You are very brave. It is not easy to close your eyes and trust someone else to take care of you. Who would like to be next?" Take each child who wants to, repeating the process.

Extensions: Allow children to blind walk you after you have blind walked them.

Make the paths more intricate.

Note: This is really very scary as you will note when someone takes you on a blind walk.

Fantasy

During the years of three and four, many children express themselves through fantasies and dramatic play. Commonly there will be a drama taking place in the active play area as a superhero sweeps down and vanquishes all who come before him, and then himself falls victim to some great force more powerful than even he. In the sandbox, there may be a quiet session of cake baking or tea preparation. At times the stories and the themes are truly frightening to the observing adult. The fantasies speak clearly of the child's fears and hopes. Often they are very close to our own. Being the most powerful person on earth, respected and feared by all, is something any one of us may have fantasized about in one guise or another. Who of us had not longed to assume the authority and control which our parents possessed as they confidently prepared a meal or cleaned the house? Wishing to be a baby again, particularly if there is another baby in the house, is a common fantasy among children—to be the center of attention and have everything taken care of. These fantasies have meaning for many of us. Acting out such fantasies is often very satisfying.

Fantasies provide a framework for movement and an opportunity to communicate with children on another level. In building a fantasy with a group of children, the teacher is recognizing the value of fantasies. If the themes of the fantasies relate to the children's own fantasies, the teacher is saying, "I have those same dreams. I think it's important to act them out too. I understand that you have these fears and wishes. You aren't alone."

Folk tales, like "Jack and the Bean Stalk" and "The Three Billy Goats Gruff" have been and are popular because they deal with common wishes and fears. They are a rich source of material for fantasy work. Feel free to modify them for your group of children. Folk tales should reflect the teller and the audience. The teller is free to add and take away parts of the tale. The folk tale must be of interest to the teller, however, in order to be successful.

Other sources of material are stories that have special interest to the children, conversations of children, fantasies you see the children acting out spontaneously, and problems you suspect the children might want to explore because of occurrences in their lives.

Fantasies can be built with young three-year-old children during free play times. The theme will be simple and may continue for some time or be over in a minute. As children mature, they gain in their ability to immerse themselves in another reality. Many four-year-olds are able to become totally absorbed by the role they are playing. They can carry young three-year-olds along with them because of the power of their fantasies, though the younger children may not understand the intensity of the older children.

In the development of a fantasy, reality can change rapidly. In the example given below, the participants change from trees into birds. Changing roles with ease is part of fantasizing. It is also possible to repeat activities over and over just because the activity is interesting, as we do in the example when we pounce for the snake twice.

Remember to include ideas from the class as you build the fantasy. Ask the children questions during the process and let their answers determine the path the fantasy takes. This is essential in maintaining involvement of the children.

A period of high activity and a period of gentleness within each fantasy provide contrast in movement which adds to the vitality of the activity.

Begin the fantasy with the children in their separate spaces so that they have a chance to become absorbed individually by the fantasy before they begin working with others. During the fantasy, children sometimes come together and at other times they can be apart. If the children end up in various spaces on the floor, the teacher can end the class with a short stroking of the back. If the fantasy has been successful, there is a lovely, satisfying feeling in stopping the session at the end of the fantasy. It will have woven a spell which all will savor in the return to real life.

Possible elements to include when creating a fantasy are being powerful, escaping, taking a trip, death, serious injury, fire, earthquake, robbers, swimming, hiding, being an animal, caring for someone, being angry, being mean, feeling sad, being a baby, being a parent, being lost, losing a parent.

As a teacher you have an opportunity for instruction. You can act out what to do if there is a fire in the house; you can be clear about the permanence of death and talk about different beliefs on the subjects; you can explore what it feels like to be lost and what to do if it happens. Always remember: *it is important in fantasies to start out from a safe place and to end up in a safe place.*

A Nature Fantasy

Objectives: To explore movement. To feel what it is like to be a part of nature.

Considerations: Four-year-olds are ready for this kind of work. Three-year-olds can take part with four-year-olds, but a young three-year-old group usually needs to wait.

Directions: "I want everyone down on the floor curled up like this." Curl up with your knees on the floor. "You are now a seed, buried down inside the ground. The rain is going to come down and land on your backs and when it does, you are very, very slowly going to begin to grow." Gently tap each person's back with your fingers. "You are slowly reaching up for the sun, slowly, slowly, slowly reaching for the sun until you are a tall beautiful tree with long branches that move gently in the gentle wind. There you are swaying gently in the wind—swaying back and forth, back and forth. But now the wind is getting stronger. It's making your branches really move around. Your branches are moving so hard that you've got to move; and you know what? You've changed into a bird and now you're flying. You're flying up and down and all around because the wind is blowing you so hard, you're just being swept all around. Fly. Fly. Fly. Oh, but now you remember you left baby back in its nest so let's fly back to the nest over here and see if our baby's all right. Here it is, but it looks sad. What do you think it wants!" Choose an answer from those offered. "Food? What kind of food do you think this kind of bird eats?" Again, choose an answer from those offered. "Snakes? Well we must be hawks then. Let's go find a snake. Fly around and look. Fly and fly and look and look. Aha! I see one way down there. We've got to dive down fast now and pounce! Ready? Pounce! Let's do that again. Stand up and pounce! Great. We've got our snake; let's fly back to our baby. We can carry the snake in our mouths. Let's fly back. Fly. Fly. Fly back to our baby. Look how happy the baby is to see us. Yummy, yummy dinner. Let's everybody eat. Yum, yum. Do I like snake. Oh, I think it's time to sleep." Stretch. "Let's all find a nice place to sleep. Curl up tight and go to sleep. It's been a big day. It feels so good to sleep."

Notes: The children operate in their separate spaces until they come to the nest where the baby bird is. They can then either stay together as a group or separate as they look for the snake and pounce. At the end they may separate again to go to sleep.

This is an example of a fantasy I have done. You must create your own.

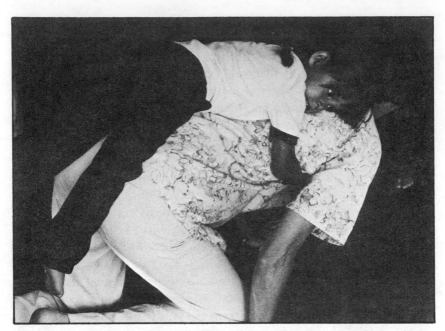

The younger child's transition can be eased by making it a pleasurable process. This child is riding to where she will put on her shoes.

Ending the session

Each of the three endings suggested here ends the session with a different feeling. A relaxation creates a feeling of individual calmness and connection with the teacher. A song game generates a feeling of being a part of a group that enjoys working together. If children do their favorite movement for each other, there is a feeling of personal validation, and sometimes a sense of personal creativity.

The teacher's choice of which way to end the session should be determined by personal preference. The activity used to end the session can vary or it can be a dependable ritual. If the same ending is not done at the end of each session, the choice of endings can be based upon what happened in the group that day. The teacher can decide which feeling she or he would like to leave with the group.

If the younger children resist stopping, you can give them a ride on your back to their shoes. Go down on your hands and knees and put yourself as close to the ground as you can so they can climb on. Do not put your head and shoulders down and your hips up, or your back will be at a slant. The child should climb on your back and lie down with the belly to your back. Rise up and crawl to the shoes. Encourage the child to stay on until you have lowered yourself to the floor again and rolled to the side so that the child can easily roll off.

Song games

Choose a song game from the section on bringing the group together (p. 39), or use a favorite song game of your own. My favorite is *"Old Lady Sally"* because the song and game delight me and because I like the settling effect of the bow at the end.

Doing Your Favorite Movement

Objectives: To learn to identify what you like to do. To be able to perform for others.

Consideration: The floor crossings format is used (p. 60).

Directions: "I would like everyone sitting down over on this side of the room with me. For our last activity today, I would like each of you to stop and think. What has been your favorite movement to do in this class? Really think. What did you really like doing today? I'll give you a minute. OK, raise your hand if you are ready and would like to show us what your favorite movement is. Ronnie. Now let's watch and see what Ronnie likes to do most. She likes to crawl super fast across the floor. That's great, Ronnie. Now I'd like you to sit on the other side of the room behind the line so that you can watch the others."

Extensions: The teacher might specify that the children do their very best jumps or sideways movement depending upon what activities had been done in class that day.

Notes: The teacher may want to say, "Do your favorite movement, except no somersaults." That is often a favorite movement but most children need help in tucking their heads, and until they learn to tuck properly somersaults are a painful affair.

Centering

Objectives: To feel solid and calm inside. To know tactually where different parts of the body are. To create an individual teacher-child connection.

Directions: "Everyone needs to lie down on the floor on your back. Feel the floor under you. It is very solid and safe and takes good care of you. Now I am going to come around and touch each one of you on your shoulders. After I touch you, you can get up and begin putting your shoes on. I'll be over to help you when I have touched everyone. Now let me see who looks really ready. Who is really relaxed and ready to have me come touch them? Keith, I am touching your shoulders now. I'm going to give the shoulder muscles a little massage. They worked so hard swinging your arms around and holding you up when you bucked. You did nice work today. I liked the way you rolled Sandy across the floor. You know how to be so gentle. You may go put your shoes on now."

Extensions: Rub different parts of the body, for example, the legs, spine, head, arms, chest, or hips.

Use some of the strength-and-groundedness activities (p. 71) such as trying to pull the child up, lifting the curled-up child, pushing against the curled-up child. The activities where children are not moved along the floor and where they do not interact with others are the ones to use.

Ask the children to be loose and limp like a piece of wet spaghetti. Lift the arms and legs gently to test them. Lift under the knees and elbows so they do not hurt themselves when the limb drops back to the floor.

Notes: Most children really enjoy being touched by the teacher and talked to in a special way. You are probably not going to be able to say all of the things that were said to Keith because you will need to move more quickly from child to child, but this gives you an idea of the kinds of things you might say. If you say to one child that she or he did nice work, you should point out something positive to all children, though you can add your expectations. For example, "Nichole, I like your energy, but next time I want you to sit down right away when I ask you to and not fool around. OK?"

Additional ending-the-session activities

Rocks (p. 77)
Turn Me Not (p. 78)
Staying Together (p. 80)
Lazy Sways (p. 86)
Resting (p. 87)
Falling (p. 88)
Fantasy (p. 92)

Part III: A Movement Program for Five- to Eight-Year-Old Children

Chapter 4: Techniques for planning and teaching sessions

The activities within this part of the book are designed for teacher-directed movement sessions. This should be just one component of the movement or physical education program for this age group. It is assumed that children have free play periods and that traditional physical education activities are also offered to the children.

The material which follows is divided into two chapters. This first chapter describes techniques for teaching and planning the sessions. The rationale for the organization of material and an explanation of the subject matter are also given. The second chapter consists of activities arranged in approximate order of difficulty.

Grouping the children

Most of the activities in this part of the book are one of three types: for individuals, for partners, or for group participation. An enormous contrast in the texture of the session can be achieved easily by altering the structure of the children's working situation. This contrast in texture is of vital importance in maintaining children's interest in the material. Their interest can be sustained for a long period of time if there is variety in the kind of concentration expected. Working by yourself, working with a partner, and working as a member of a group easily provide this variety.

Working as an individual

When a child works as an individual, she or he is in complete control. The focus of the child can be very internal. Even if the child chooses to imitate another child, that is a personal decision for which the child assumes total artistic responsibility.

Working alone on a movement problem provides an opportunity for creative exploration of a child's own movement potential. The child is unhampered by other people's needs. The child can bend mind and body to new points.

In individual work it is necessary to set conditions that allow the child to be absorbed in the problem. In many of the activities in this book there are two elements for the child to consider. Concentrating on one element will hold interest for only a brief time, whereas two elements will be more of a challenge.

Individual work provides an opportunity for the teacher to address all of the elements of movement (p. 3) in depth. Where is the body in space? What shape does it make? What can the body do at these different levels? Can the body move backward in the same kind of way? What sorts of things does a person need to do to truly make the body move sideways? If a person does that same action slowly, what happens? What does it look like? What does it feel like to do something jerkily and then to do the same thing very smoothly? Where are the elbows? What sort of movement can they make? How can a face show how a person feels? How can the body show feelings?

Individual work can provide the opportunity for a child to learn the answers to these questions in a protected environment.

When activities presented in this section produce interesting results, dividing the class, so that half can watch the other half at work, is suggested. When this is done in a matter-of-fact way performing becomes a natural process. Being watched by others can become less threatening and another step can be taken toward becoming more comfortable inside our bodies.

Working as a partner

When children work with a partner, they can be responsible for a portion of what happens, but their input must combine with and accommodate the input of the partner. The child must adjust to the reality of that person's physical capabilities and to the personal interaction that the partners develop. For most children, doing body work with a partner is a new challenge which will absorb them.

Work with a partner provides a special opportunity for people to learn more about themselves. Developing a relationship with one other person is very different from working by yourself or in a group. Each partner has a commitment and responsibility to the other for a particular period of time. Within that time the partners must learn to take a problem and to solve it in a way that is satisfactory to themselves and the other person. In society, functioning in groups and individually is stressed, more than the partner-type, one-to-one relationship. Learning to relate on a one-to-one basis is a skill which comes more easily to some than to others. In partner work, this skill is addressed directly and children are helped to learn more about themselves and their relationship to one another.

Children can learn more about their own strength and connection with the ground when this strength is challenged by another child's strength and weight. Children can learn more about how much they can trust another person by the way in which the other takes care of them. Children can learn how to develop another's trust in them by learning to take care of others. When children are taken care of, they learn what others do for them that feels good. They can try doing those same things for others and can learn how it feels to perform those actions.

In addition to the self-awareness and social awareness possibilities, there are movement possibilities that are unique to partner work. Each of these exercises deals with movement potential and the development of a greater consciousness of what shapes our bodies can form in space.

Children can either work with the same partner throughout or change partners with each new element introduced. If they work with the same partner throughout they have an opportunity to develop a more intense relationship with that person. If they change partners frequently, they are able to experience and compare the differences between people.

Sometimes children will be hesitant about being with someone of the opposite sex. If partners are changed frequently, this is less threatening. Changing partners frequently means also that no one has to be with one classmate exclusively for a long period of time. A faster pace is created by changing partners often as opposed to staying with one person where a concentration can develop. Both arrangements have advantages and can be used in different sessions depending on objectives for that session. For example, when the children seem to be moving slowly, changing partners more frequently can change the pace, or when they feel scattered, having partners stay together for a longer period of time may enhance focusing.

Working as a member of a group

When children are members of a group, their decisions must be based upon a group consciousness. The individual no longer has total control over what happens.

Working as a part of a group can be a rich experience. The combined energy of participants can create a strength surpassing that of an individual both physically and emotionally. Working with others gives children a sense of the role they can play in society as a whole. For example, a child working with other children can move another child and even an adult. By combining strengths and wills, children demonstrate graphically their ability to work with others in order to solve a problem and to alter the environment.

In these group activities, children can also become aware of the community structures that they can create with just their bodies. The shapes and sounds created by a group of people working together have a very special quality. Ritualized dances and chants are examples of such activities. Rituals can create powerful feelings within the participants. The feelings reflect power and belonging, that is, membership in a group and unity with others.

Many children have difficulty in being a part of a group. The intimacy which a group demands and the giving up of self which occurs when contributing to a group effort are threatening prospects for some. Such children need time to watch others performing group activities. They need to observe the rich rewards of group activitities such as pride in group accomplishment and unique experiences.

The activities in this book are for groups of different sizes. In some activities, the class should be divided into small groups and in other activities the entire class can participate. A suggested group size will be noted with each activity.

Subject matter considerations

Most of the activities in this part of the book deal with movement and body awareness, strength and groundedness, trust and sensitivity, or fantasy. Additionally, there are activities which are grouped together because they are best for either beginning or ending a session.

Each session should be planned to include activities from several of these categories. The subject matter will become more integrated into the children's lives if they receive a constant, low-pressure exposure rather than a concentrated heavy dose. The emphasis of the sessions may flow more strongly in one direction for a period of time, but an attempt should be made to include all of these categories often.

Movement and body awareness

The activities in this category often generate a high, bouncy energy which can make movement sessions joyful for children. These are the traditional activities of dance. They concentrate on the development of the body skills, the development of an awareness of body image and body mechanics, and the development of body expression. These activities are not emotionally demanding of the children because the focus is generally on body mechanics rather than on feelings.

Strength and groundedness

These activities tend to be settling. They feel good. Children feel a strong connection with the ground; it is one thing in life they can always count on. They have spent a lot of time on the ground exploring it as infants and toddlers, playing on it with their friends. The ground is close to children physically and emotionally. Children love tactile stimulation; the ground provides this stimulation when children roll on it or slither across it. Strength is related to groundedness in that children's strength is greatest when their connection with the ground is firm. When children push against something their support comes from the ground, and if the lines of support are strong and true then the strength is greater. Feeling such strength gives a sense of power that is reassuring and centering.

Trust and sensitivity

These activities are challenging emotionally to children. When they are first introduced, some children will find them uncomfortable. They ask for a level of sophistication in the child's development where the child is able to theorize how another person is feeling. It is important to introduce the concept of caring and the concept that children's behavior affects other people, just as the behavior of other people affects them. Trust and sensitivity activities can be used in ways which reflect the developmental level of a group. If the children are older and have been together as a group for a period of time, more time can be given to this type of activity. If the group is younger and children have not known one another very long, it would be better to wait until they have been together for a while before making use of this material. Lead up to the introduction of trust and sensitivity activities by emphasizing similar caring aspects in other activities, particularly those on strength and groundedness.

Fantasy

In building a fantasy with a group of children the teacher has an opportunity to enter their world, to join them in exploring the unknown, the frightening, and the absurd. In building fantasies the teacher formalizes the dramatic play of children, thereby validating it and encouraging its expression at other times. Fantasizing is a very important part of the human spirit which helps us all arrive at a better understanding of our world. Adults most often fantasize in their heads. Children often fantasize with their bodies—acting out all that they imagine.

Fantasies are a time when teachers can truly apply their own creative instincts. However, truly creative adults can allow the fantasies of the children to grow over the framework they, as teachers, provide.

The teacher should also keep in mind, during fantasy activities, ways of applying and extending the content explored in other sections of the movement sessions.

Beginning a session

The first activity of a session should be something fun, active, that creates a group energy, and that poses a challenge. It can always be the same, thus a ritual to look forward to. The main objectives should be to warm up the body, to leave self-consciousness behind, and to generate an enthusiastic spirit.

An activity that warms up the body is one in which rapid movement occurs. Most children enjoy running or jumping and so incorporating running or jumping into this first activity is an easy and appropriate way of warming up—of getting the heart beating and the blood flowing. The structures of these activities are firm so that the excitement of the movement can be easily controlled.

Leaving self-consciousness behind happens when children are working individually in a situation where they are not watching one another. If there is a high degree of activity or concentration required, then the children will be so busy that they will not be confronting each other.

Ending a session

These activities relax and center the children. They are designed so that the children can retreat to their individual worlds and prepare themselves for moving on into the rest of the day. They bring the children down so they can move on more easily.

Being able to relax, being able to let the tensions flow out of the body, is a valuable skill. The teacher should take time to allow development of this section. Touching helps some children understand this part of the session more. The tone and touch of the teacher are vital to the success of this part of the session. Everyone should be able to leave with a sense of well-being.

Pacing a session

In every area of teaching, the art of pacing is critical: being able to sense what comes next; knowing that the children are coming to the end of their involvement with one activity and that it is time to change to another; knowing that the activity you have chosen is not working and that you should just leave it (another day or another time it might be right, but not at this moment). Children let you know quickly when you have their interest and when you do not. If several children seem to have tried out your direction and are looking distracted, it is probably time to add to the direction or move to something new. Children will communicate their interest by working with the material rather than developing little games with friends, and by readily giving attention when addressed.

If children find a problem absorbing, then it should be continued until attention begins to wane. You may choose to bring that same activity back at the next meeting with a variation or extension.

Sometimes the children request a repetition of an activity. When this happens, give strong consideration to deviating from the plan to acknowledge the request. It is important to be responsive to the children's ideas.

At the end of an activity, it is important to occasionally provide space for discussion. Children will naturally want to discuss new discoveries. You may want to ask them how a particular activity felt. This is a time when you can acquire information directly from them about what is happening.

Providing variety and contrast

Sessions need to be varied in texture and content so that

children's interest is sustained. In choosing activities it is important to contrast the following:

1. Activities in which interaction with other people is demanded and activities where the child is able to work independently.
2. High-energy activities with grounding, slowly paced activities.
3. Activities that have imagery with those that are more abstract.
4. Activities in which things are tightly defined with activities where there is more freedom of expression.
5. Activities that demand physical control with those that are more free flowing.
6. Activities where concentration is required with those that are less exacting.
7. Activities that will be developed for a stretch of time with those that will be completed quickly.
8. Activities with high emotional content with activities that are primarily physical.

In selecting activities it would be difficult to include all of these contrasts every time; these are some variations to keep in mind in planning each session. The activities in this guide have been grouped to reflect some of these contrasts, so that simply choosing from several categories will assure variety.

Making a plan

Before doing a movement session with children, it is necessary to make a list of the activities that would help you most in achieving your goals for your specific group. Base your choices on the information in Part I and in this section, combined with knowledge of the group you will work with. Factors to consider include these:

- age of the group
- size of the group
- length of time the group has been together

- general feeling of the group
- size and condition of the space
- amount of time allotted
- kind of content appropriate for this session
- promises to the children for activities they have requested

Choose an activity from those for beginning a session (p. 113). After excess energy has been expended during the first activity, the children should be able to concentrate easily on one of the activities for individuals (p. 117) or for partners (p. 125). If this will be a long class session, choose an activity from each category.

The fantasy material (p. 145) offers a good change of pace at this point. Be certain to have a theme prepared. Then, depending upon the time available, choose an activity for group participation (p. 138) that brings the members of the class together, and do a relaxation activity for ending the session (p. 149), or just do a relaxation.

Natural transitions can be provided during the activities by ending one activity that shares a beginning point with another, particularly if the children are on the floor. For example, end an activity on the floor and have the children roll to an appropriate space for an activity that begins on the floor.

This will comprise the basic plan for the class. Be ready to be flexible. Your intuition about the children's mood is the most important ingredient, and it may cause you to change the order of activities, extend the first activity far longer than you expected, drop an activity immediately after its introduction, or go in a completely new direction not covered in this guide, but which you feel is valid and appropriate for that day. The activities suggested here are resources upon which to draw during the period of time committed to working with the children. Trust yourself and your knowledge of teaching to know when to deviate from your plan.

First-session plans

The activities for the first session should include *Freeze!* (p. 115) in order to introduce the children to the word *freeze* as a control word, and in order to introduce them to *shapes* which is a concept integral to movement and body awareness work. Activities demanding intense concentration or that require closeness with other people are best saved for later sessions. In the first session, plan with an eye for enjoyment.

Preparing the class

Prior to beginning the session, you would be wise to inform the children about what will be happening. Children need to know the following information:

- what is going to happen
- where it will happen
- the schedule
- what is expected of them during the activity
- what sorts of clothing changes they will make

Allow time before, during, and after the class for children to ask questions and discuss their reactions.

What lies ahead

Doing movement classes is a challenge that has great rewards for the teacher. Success and failure should be expected. These classes, which challenge every skill of a teacher, produce a special kind of energy. Use it and experiment constantly to make the material work for you.

Chapter 5: Movement sessions for older children

Activities for beginning a session

Going

Objectives: To enjoy using body in different locomotions. To explore varieties of locomotion.

Considerations: A room with open space between two walls. This activity works well with five- and six-year-old children.

Directions: "Let's run together to that wall. Now let's run together to the other wall. Now let's walk like robots really stiffly to that wall."

At this time incorporate any of the movement elements (p. 61) such as: moving backward, sideways, loosely like a scarecrow, or in slow motion; galloping; skipping; turning around the whole way; or making curvy paths.

Notes: These should never become races. You are just moving from one wall to another. There are no winners.

Names

Objectives: To experience pleasure in creating group sound and movement. To develop a sense of group intimacy.

Consideration: Can be done in a limited space.

Directions: "Everyone come in close and squat on the floor. We are going to count to 10 and clap our hands. When I say '10' everyone jump into the air and call your name. Your own name.

Ready? 1, 2, 3, 4, 5, 6, 7, 8, 9, 10, Molly." Repeat several times.

Extensions: Whisper names. Call each person's name in turn. Say silly words like *hamburger.* Make a meaningless sound like a whoop or pshhhhh.

Note: You will have to remind the class of the difference between calling and shouting or screaming.

The Snake

Objectives: To enjoy various forms of locomotion. To acquire enough control to maintain place in group. To acquire ability to lead a group. To understand the concept of *paths.*

Consideration: Can be done in a limited space.

Directions: Clap your hands as you begin walking. "Follow me exactly in a single line so that we look like a big snake, and I am the head." Walk in a pattern that is easily followed. Begin moving more quickly until you are jogging. As you do movements, the children in the line behind you will imitate you. Explore various movement elements (p. 61) as you move, describing them as you do: "Now I am moving very lightly. Now I am very heavy." The class should be moving in one long line that makes a curved path in, and around, the room.

Extensions: Allow children to lead the line. Suggest directions regarding movement element extensions.

Notes: You will need to be the first leader. Skill is required by the leader not to lose the body of the snake. Older children may be able to follow a direction such as, "Make the snake as curvy as possible."

Freeze!

Objectives: To enjoy movement and shape making. To explore varieties of locomotion and shapes.

Considerations: Can be done in a limited space. A drum is useful.

Directions: "I am going to count from 1 to 10. While I am count-ing you can move as much as you want. When I reach 10 I will say 'Freeze!' and you should freeze in a shape."

Once you establish the form, you can specify either what the movement should be like or what the shape should be like. The movement variations can be: level, speed, direction (backward, sideways), quality (floppily, shakily, stiffly). The shape variations you ask for when the children freeze can specify: level, quality, emotional quality (horrible, beautiful), connected to someone else.

Extension: Do collapses to the floor instead of freezes.

Note: Move this exercise along quickly so that no shape is seen as precious.

Contrasts

Objectives: To enjoy movement freedom. To acquire control of behavior.

Considerations: Can be done in a limited space. A drum is useful. Have two sounds prepared.

Directions: Have two different sounds. You can use your voice or an instrument. "When I make this sound you are a monster." Make your first sound. "When I make this sound you are a sweetiepie." Make your second sound. Alter the length of time

you make each sound. Sometimes change sounds rapidly; sometimes continue one sound for a while.

Extensions: Slow motion/fast motion; high level/low level;
backward/forward; stiff motion/fluid motion; angry/happy;
sloppy/neat; small movements/large movements.

Places

Objective: To acquire an awareness of a point in space and a
point in time.

Considerations: Ample space is required. A drum is useful. This
activity is appropriate for older children.

Directions: "Pick out a place in the room with your eyes. Now
walk to that place. Look around. Can you remember exactly
where you are? Now pick out another place in the room with your
eyes. Walk to that place. Freeze. Look around. Remember this
place. Now walk back to the first place. Freeze. Now walk back to
the second place. Freeze in a shape when you are there. Now I
will count to 5 and I want you to arrive at Place 1 exactly when I
reach 5, not before or after. 1, 2, 3, 4, 5. Freeze! Now move to your
other place backward while I count to 5. Not before or after. 1, 2, 3,
4, 5. Freeze!"

Extensions: Moving from place to place in slow motion, in fast
motion, at high level, at middle level, at low level, backward,
sideways, stiffly, fluidly, angrily, happily, galloping, jumping,
hopping, sliding, shuffling, etc.
   You can add a third place when children have mastered moving between two places.

Activities for individuals: movement and body awareness

Faces

Objective: To become aware of the movement potential of the face, and of its expressive qualities.

Consideration: Can be done in a limited space.

Directions: "Let's see what we can do with our faces. First of all give your face a good rub all over. Doesn't that feel good? Now let's see what your face looks like when you're eating something really good. Yum! Yum! Oh! It's turned very sticky. It's kind of hard to open your mouth. You look very worried. Oh, now everything is OK, but it's getting kind of boring just chewing and chewing. Now it's become very sour. Oh. What a horrible taste! Terrible! Thank goodness. Now it's gone away. Now you feel just fine."

Extensions: Any kind of qualitative element you can dream up, such as sorrow, baby face, skinniness, surprise.
   Add sounds to the expression.

Note: Divide the group in half for this activity so that one group can perform for the other.

Knees

Objectives: To become aware of the importance of the knee joint. To see variety of movement the knee joint makes possible.

Consideration: Can be done in a limited space.

Directions: "Have you ever thought about your knees? They are wonderful joints. Let's give them a pat. You can beat a little rhythm on your knees with different parts of your hands. Spend a minute trying out what sounds you can make and finding a rhythm you like." You can share some if there is interest.

"What do your knees do? You can kind of make them disappear, can't you? Let's practice bending and unbending them. There are different ways you can make them bend and unbend. Let's try some different ones." Try squats, lying on your back, walking with the knees coming up high. "How can you move if your knees are stuck together? How can you move if your knees are way far apart? Now let's try to move our knees really fast while we are moving with them far apart. And make them move really fast when they are where they usually are. Knees are amazing! Let's sit down and give them a little rest. Let's stroke them and let them know how important they are to us."

Extensions: Walk on your knees, walk in a low crouch, have the knees talk to other people's knees, have the knees move toward and away from one another, or crawl on your stomach and have your knees come close to your ears.

Do this activity with other joints.

Notes: The knees are the most versatile body part with which to do this activity, but it is interesting to contrast the movement of other body parts to the knees.

Sliding

Objectives: To experience the pleasure of the free flow movement of sliding. To acquire the skill of sliding and an awareness of the shape of the body in space.

Considerations: Ample space with a smooth floor is required. Each child must wear socks. A drum is useful.

Directions: Divide the group in half. One half sits and watches while the other group slides.

"We are going to experiment with running and sliding." (After a reasonable period of time, switch groups.) "Now come to this end of the room. I want the first group to run to that end of the room, but before you get there, begin your slide and arrange your body in a shape. Freeze when you stop." After everyone has frozen in a shape, make comments to the watchers about the varieties of shapes. "Now run back this way and give us a grand slide in another shape and freeze. Be careful not to crash into us." Then reverse the groups.

Extension: After the children slide, ask if they can fall and roll.

Note: This is also a good warm-up activity.

Collapsing

Objectives: To master the collapse. To acquire control of the tension level in the body.

Considerations: Can be done in a limited space. A drum is useful.

Directions: "Find a place on the floor and stand there. Make sure you have some space around you. Now make your body very stiff and tight and when I clap my hands I want you to let go immediately of the stiffness and collapse to the floor like a wet noodle." Clap. "Relax. Feel the shape your body makes on the floor. Now rise in slow motion. Make your body stiff and hard again." Clap. "Relax. Collapse onto the floor. Feel the floor under you."

Repeat the exercise several times.

Extensions: Children can rise in different manners: smoothly, jerkily, staccato, twisting.

The class can be divided and one half can watch the other half perform.

Note: Emphasize the contrast between tension and lack of tension.

Jumping Shapes

Objectives: To acquire thé skill of running and jumping and running. To explore the varieties of shapes possible.

Considerations: Ample space is required. A drum is useful.

Directions: "Find a place in the room and become a statue. Make a shape, and freeze in that shape. I will clap my hands five times and while I am clapping, I want you to change in slow motion to another shape. 1, 2, 3, 4, 5. Freeze!"
Continue the procedure, asking for shapes that are stretched out, small, full of action, very relaxed, where just one part of the body changes. If you need to, have the shape changes come quickly. First you are one way and then instantly another way, changing from one stretched-out shape to another new stretched-out shape.
After the children have experimented with a wide range of shapes, bring them to one side of the room. "Now I want you to run to the center of the room, one by one, jump up and make a shape, and keep on running to the other side of the room."
Suggest qualities for the shapes.

Extension: Children run toward each other from opposite sides of the room and when they are near the middle they jump and make a shape to each other.

Paths

Objectives: To acquire knowledge of the shape of a path made by the body. To learn how to avoid collisions.

Considerations: A clean, smooth floor and ample space are required. This activity is appropriate for older children.

Directions: "Everyone lie down on their backs on the floor. Now let me see the different ways that you can move while you are lying on your back. Be careful of other people. I don't want any crashes. ... Freeze! That was good. Some people like to move rapidly and some people like to move more slowly, but you were all taking really good care of each other. Now, I want you to make only straight paths—no curves. Go. Straight paths. ... Freeze! That was good. Now this time, I want only curvy paths. I don't want to see a straight path anywhere on the floor. Let me see you go. Curves, curves, curves. ... Freeze! That was excellent. This time my voice will tell you whether to make a curvy path or a straight path. Curve. Curve. Curve. Curve. Curve. Straight. Straight. Straight. Curve. Curve." Continue, but watch carefully. Allow the children to feel comfortable with the changes in paths before making the timing of the changes more challenging.

Extensions: Allow a child to call the directions of "curve" and "straight."
   Divide the group in half so that they can watch one another.
   Use different methods of locomotion such as walking, marching, sliding, and tip-toeing with the differentiation of the curved paths from the straight ones.

Focus

Objectives: To acquire control of eye focus. To become aware of the existence and use of eye focus.

Considerations: Ample space is required. A drum is useful. This activity is appropriate for seven- and eight-year-old children.

Directions: "Find a space to stand somewhere in the room. With your eyes choose a spot in another part of the room. Look at that spot. Point at it and walk to it. Now find another spot in the room with your eyes, focus on that spot, point to it, and run to it. Find another spot, focus on it, point, and run again to it. Focus on another spot, point to it. Do you see it clearly? Hop to it looking at it the entire time. Focus on a new spot. Point. Skip. Focus on a new spot. Point. Gallop. Focus. Point. Run. Focus. Point. Skate. Focus. Point. Run. Collapse."

Extension: Use other types of locomotion (p. 61).

Notes: This activity demands an abstract conceptualization of space which only seven- or eight-year-old children should be challenged to do. The spot which they choose to go to must be chosen by them. Once chosen, the spot becomes concrete.

Activities for individuals: strength and groundedness

Growing

Objectives: To understand the relationship of the body to the ground. To acquire a sense of the essence of growth and its relationship to the ground.

Consideration: Ample space is required.

Directions: "Lie on your backs and curl up so that you can rock back and forth. Rocking. Rocking. Rocking. And now roll over onto your hands and knees and feel what it feels like to crawl. Crawl in and out of all of these other crawlers. Crawl backward, forward, sideways, slow, fast, close to other people, and way far away from them. And now you are getting bigger, you use your arms and legs to get around. Your arms and hands are as strong as your legs and feet. Give them weight just as though they were your legs and feet.

You are a real four-legged person now. Moving really low like an ape. Let's see you leap up and land in a crouch. You are like some wonderful wild animal. Now you rest, now you leap. Now you are growing taller and your leaps are very light. You are running lightly and leaping whenever you feel like it. You are like a feather, running, and leaping. And now one last leap and down you go to the ground where you began. Feel the ground under your body, holding you up. Feel your breath going down to the center of your body."

Note: This activity is important for the strong sense of the ground it conveys to the child.

Balance and Fall

Objectives: To understand personal body weight and momentum. To acquire the ability to balance and fall easily. To develop a relationship with the ground which continues as the body leaves the ground.

Considerations: Ample space is required. This activity is appropriate for older children.

Directions: "Lie on your back on the ground. Now roll onto your side and let yourself fall back onto your back. Again, on the other side. Roll onto your side. Balance. And now fall back onto the ground."
    Repeat several times.
    "Now curl up, still lying on your back. Can you roll onto your seat? Let's see if your body can be like a ball rolling back and forth from your shoulders to your seat. Where are the good balancing places? What if you balance in the middle? What happens? Be sure to keep your head tucked. Now stand on your knees. Can you drop to the floor and do a roll and come back up to your knees? Balance. And now go back down and up. Balance."

See if the children can fall from a standing position, and then roll and stand up.

Extension: Once the children have acquired the skills involved, accompany them with your voice or a drum.

Notes: The first part of this exercise can be done easily. Take the children only as far in the exercise as they are able to go. It progresses to a fairly sophisticated level.

Activities for individuals: trust and sensitivity

Sounds and Shapes

Objectives: To unite sound with body movement. To recognize the unity of sound and body movement.

Consideration: Can be done in a limited space.

Directions: "Find a space in the center of the room. I am going to say a word. With your body and your voice, but no words, make a shape and a sound that goes with the shape. Strong. Now another word. Gentle. Good. That one was harder, wasn't it? Heavy. Let me see you move and your sound should be a part of your movement. You are heavy. Let me see and hear your heaviness."

Other qualities: shaky, oily, tiny, huge, shy, scared, mad, beautiful, ugly.

Extensions: Divide the group in half so children may watch one another.

Have the children make sounds that are made with the breath

alone—no voice, like "shhh," hisses, "ch-ch-ch, tsk-tsk," etc.

Have the children make sounds that are only voice sounds—no breath sounds.

Activities for partners: movement and body awareness

Two-Headed Creature

Objectives: To have two people work out how to move as one. To acquire an awareness of the movement and shape possibilities of two bodies combined in space.

Consideration: Can be done in a limited space.

Directions: "I would like you and your partner to find a way to be connected while you move across the floor at your lowest level. Try to become like one creature all connected."

Repeat this exercise at the middle level, at the highest level, in slow motion, very fast, moving backward, moving sideways.

Extensions: Use any of the movement elements on page 61, such as those above, for example: twisting, jabbing, shaking, all relaxed, all stiff.

Notes: Children need to spend time developing their creatures. They should be given the opportunity to show them to one another.

Statues

Objectives: To acquire an understanding of body shape and how joints work. To be sensitive to another person's body.

Consideration: Can be done in a limited space.

Directions: "One of you is to be a statue and the other is the sculptor. Now, sculptor, arrange the statue in a shape that you like. Do this with your hands and body as much as possible."
    You can have this done at a specified level: low, middle, high; or with a specified emotional quality: angry, happy, funny, scared, scary; or with a motional quality: outstretched, twisted, balanced, in the middle of a movement.

Extensions: Sculpting the statue without using hands.
    Once the statues have been formed, the sculptors sit down and the statues move as their shapes would dictate.

Mirrors

Objectives: To become aware of the shape of the body. To understand the role of the leader and to be responsible for another body's movement.

Consideration: Can be done in a limited space.

Directions: The total class should face you.
    "I am going to do some movements and I would like you to copy me exactly." Do simple movements that can be easily followed.
    "Now, choose a partner. Sit facing each other. One person will be the leader and the other person will follow. The person who leads needs to move only one or two body parts at a time. You

want your partner to be able to follow." After a time, switch leaders.

Extensions: Once the children can lead and follow with only one or two body parts moved, they can begin to lead with their whole body.

Note: Attention span is limited for this intense activity.

Conversations

Objectives: To isolate the use of one body part. To be sensitive to another. To acquire control of motions.

Considerations: Can be done in a limited space. This activity is appropriate for older children.

Directions: "Stand or sit facing one another. Using only your hands and fingers, have a conversation with your partner. First one of you talks and then the other. Now use your face. No words. First one talks and then the other. Are you listening to what the other person says? Don't decide what you're going to do until your partner is finished. And now say something to your partner with your whole body. And now freeze. Partner, you reply with your whole body."

Extensions: Have the children use other body parts: feet, elbows, shoulders, head. Suggest subject matter: anger, sadness, joy, disgust, fear.

Notes: It is important that the listening partner really listen so that it becomes a true conversation and not just two people making movements *at* one another.

Gibberish

Objectives: To be sensitive to another person. To understand use of the body in language.

Considerations: Can be done in a limited space. The teacher should practice talking gibberish beforehand. This activity is appropriate for older children.

Directions: "Do you know how to talk gibberish? It sounds like this." Give an example using great expression and your whole body; speak, using no recognizable words. "Now let's all try it together." Everybody speaks gibberish. "Now I would like you to find a partner and have a gibberish conversation with her or with him. If you decide to explain something, you may have to do a lot of acting out."

Extensions: Have couples demonstrate their skill to the others. Each couple should have a chance to perform if they would like to.

Activities for partners: strength and groundedness

Pushing Backs

Objectives: To feel a personal strength and to understand how a connection with the ground is the foundation of that strength.

Considerations: Can be done in a small space. This works well with younger children.

Directions: "Sit down on the floor back to back. Now push as hard as you can against the other person's back. If the other person pushes back, what happens? If the other person doesn't push back, what happens? Take care of each other." If your floor is smooth, one partner will be able to push the other around the floor.

Children usually figure out that they can stand up together if they both push against one another's backs. However, that is only a part of this exercise. The important element is to develop a sense of your strength when opposed by another's and to feel how your relationship with the ground can work with your muscles to develop a total strength.

Notes: This is a good activity with which to begin partner work. Because you do not see your partner, there is less personal involvement.

Pushing Fronts

Objectives: To feel a personal strength and to understand how a connection with the ground is the foundation of that strength. To develop a sensitivity to a partner's strength and balance.

Consideration: Can be done in a limited space.

Directions: "Stand a little bit away from each other, face to face. Put your hands together. Now push against each other taking care not to push the other person off balance. Take care of your partner, but feel your strength and your partner's strength."

Extensions: The partners put their hands on the front of each other's shoulders and push.

The partners put their feet as far apart as they can from one another's feet.

Note: This activity can be used by an adult and child as an effective way for the child to express anger.

Pushing Feet

Objectives: To understand personal strength and its connection with the ground. To develop balance in an unusual situation. To be sensitive to a partner's needs.

Considerations: Ample space is required. Bare feet are essential.

Directions: "Lie down on your backs on the floor with your feet touching your partner's feet. Scoot your bodies toward each other a little bit. The soles of your feet should be touching the soles of your partner's feet. Now if only the soles of your feet are allowed to touch, how much can you move together and make different shapes with your bodies? You can move your bodies closer together or farther apart as you do this."

Extension: Bicycling together. However, this moves the focus from strength and groundedness to trust and sensitivity.

Rocks

Objectives: To develop a sense of strength as it comes from the ground. To be senstitive to a partner.

Consideration: Can be done in a small space.

Directions: "One partner is a solid rock. Make yourself as solid as you can on the ground. Now this rock will miraculously grow roots. It will send roots all the way down to the center of the earth. The partner will very gently push this rock. If you push a little harder the rock will have to be strong not to move. See how hard you can push without the rock moving. Let the rock feel how strong it is. Can you push your hardest and the rock still does not move? Take care of your partner. Now change places." The pushers become the rocks and the rocks become the pushers.

Extension: The pushers push with other parts of their bodies besides their hands.

Notes: The pushers must be careful not to hurt the rocks by poking or pushing in vulnerable places. Take time to develop the feeling of the roots going into the earth with each set of rocks.

The Hanging "Thing"

Objective: To devise ways to move together.

Consideration: Must be done on a smooth floor.

Directions: "One partner should be standing and the other partner is on the floor. The partner on the floor should hang onto the leg of the standing person. Now, can the standing person go anywhere with this 'thing' hanging on? All of you who are the 'thing' should not help your partner move, but you should not work to keep her or him from moving. Just relax and be there. . . . Now can you other partners move if the 'thing' hangs onto both legs? It's OK to use your hands on the floor. You might have to to get anywhere. OK. Now change positions. The 'thing' is going to be the puller and the puller is going to be the 'thing.' "
  Repeat your instructions.

Extension: The "thing" can actively help the puller move.

The Glob

Objectives: To explore ways of moving another body. To find the body's heavy points. To feel strength. To be sensitive to a partner's feelings. To be able to relax.

Consideration: This can be done on a rug, but pushing and

pulling must be eliminated if you do so.

Directions: "One partner is relaxed on the floor. No bones in that body at all. Just a big glob of body. Now the other partner will find a way of moving that glob of body very carefully. Try different ways. You can push, you can pull, you can roll. Take care of your partner."

Extension: Eliminate the use of hands. Can the children move their partners without touching them with their hands?

Note: The relaxed partner should tell the manipulator if something is hurting.

The Glob Travels

Objectives: To feel strength. To be sensitive to a partner. To develop enough trust in a partner so that the glob can relax.

Considerations: The floor must be smooth. Ample space is required.

Directions: "One person should lie on the ground. Be very relaxed. A great, big glob of body. The partner should pick up the feet of the relaxed one and pull the glob around the floor. Be careful. You need to take care of your partner and of the other people in the room. Go slowly at first. The relaxed person should say if anything becomes uncomfortable."
    Point out how relaxed those are whose bodies move loosely in response to the puller's movement. Reverse: the relaxed one becomes the puller, the puller becomes the relaxed one. Repeat the instructions.

Extensions: Pulling by the arms instead of the legs—the pulled one's head should fall back if truly relaxed.
    All go to one side of the room, and couple by couple, pull each other quickly to the other side of the room.

Turn Me Not

Objective: To feel strength and connection with the ground.

Consideration: Can be done in a limited space.

Directions: "Can you turn over someone who decides not to be turned over? Let's see. One of you should lie on the floor face down. Feel the ground under you. You are a part of the ground. Feel the roots growing out of you down into the ground. You are solid. Now, partner, very gently at first, test that strength. Try to turn that person over. I don't really want you to turn your partner over. Just test how solid your partner is. You are very strong, but your partner is very connected to the ground. OK. Now reverse positions."

Be sure to repeat the centering directions so that the prone person has a chance to become very solid.

Notes: Do not let the competitive aspects of this get out of hand. The emphasis is always on caring for the other.

If a child can be turned over easily, go and help that child learn to center resistance by talking and gently pulling in one place until the child can resist your hand's pull.

I Want Up

Objectives: To feel strength and the sources of strength. To problem solve.

Consideration: Can be done in a limited space.

Directions: "Can you get up even if someone wants to keep you on the ground? One person should lie face down on the floor. If the other person lies across your back and tries to hold you down, can you get up? Take care of each other. Do not use your hands on each other."

After a time, have the children reverse positions. Repeat the instructions.

Note: Do not let the competitive aspects of this get out of hand.

Rides

Objectives: To feel the strength necessary to support another. To develop enough trust so a partner can relax.

Consideration: Ample floor space is required.

Directions: "One partner go down on your hands and knees like you are crawling. Be still and be solid. Now the other partner very slowly and carefully arrange your whole body on top of the crawler. Are you comfortable? Arrange yourself so that you both feel comfortable. OK. Now can the bottom person transport your partner across the room? There's no hurry. Give your partner a good relaxed ride. OK. Now change positions. The person who gave the ride now gets to be carried. Take care of each other. Rider, you should arrange your whole body comfortably on your partner."

Extension: Find ways to transport each other without crawling.

Activities for partners: trust and sensitivity

The Sculptor

Objectives: To achieve enough relaxation to be molded easily. To take care of another person.

Consideration: Can be done in a limited space.

Directions: "One person is relaxed on the floor. Now the partner can arrange your body in whatever way she or he wants. You are a sculptor. The relaxed person should help the sculptor by holding the shapes the sculptor designs. Sculptor, take care of your partner."

Extension: This can also be done standing up, but the objectives become more those of body awareness than relaxation.

Balance Back

Objectives: To trust each other. To explore ways of moving. To understand weight and balance.

Consideration: Can be done in a limited space.

Directions: "Stand face to face. Now hold hands and gradually lean back. You should be balancing back. See if you can move your feet in so they are closer to your partner's feet. Are your elbows straight? You are taking care of each other. Each of you is holding the other up. Now see how you can move when you are in this position. Can you twist and bend? Can you go up and down? Take care of each other."

Usually one couple will understand the balancing. If others have difficulty understanding, direct their attention to the partners who are doing it. Make sure everyone has a chance to feel it. Some will have difficulty in letting their weight go. Make sure that the partners have a chance to experience it.

Note: Sometimes it is necessary to match partners according to size and weight.

Resting

Objectives: Feeling another person's weight. Feeling the quiet space of two people resting together.

Consideration: Can be done in a limited space.

Directions: "One person is like a rock on the floor—as solid as can be. You can either be a long skinny rock or a round rock. Now the other person should rest a hand—only a hand—on the rock. But let the rock feel the weight of just that one hand. Now rest a hand and an arm on the rock. Now rest your hand, arm, and head on the rock. Rest just the upper half of your body from your waist up on the rock. Now see how much of your body's weight you can give to the rock. The rock is strong, and it feels good to have your weight on it. Take care of the rock. And, rock, if something is uncomfortable, let your partner know. Now just rest on your rock for a little bit. Feel your partner breathe. Maybe you can feel heartbeats. Listen to the room. Relax and enjoy the feeling of your partner's body. You are taking care of each other."
Now have the rock and relaxer change roles.

Note: A good position for the rock to be in is lying down flat or really curled up in a ball with knees on the ground.

Lazy Sways

Objectives: To be able to trust another completely. To care for another. To learn how the body works.

Directions: "I would like one of you to lie on the floor on your back. Be very relaxed, like a wet piece of spaghetti. The other person should stand straddling your partner facing your part-ner's head. Like this." Demonstrate with one couple. "Lean over and firmly take hold of your partner's wrists. You will gently, very gently, lift your relaxed partner almost to a sitting position. Now gently sway the relaxed one from side to side. Slowly and gently. And now carefully lower this person back to the ground." Reverse the partners.

Notes: The explanation can be simplified by demonstrating this activity with one child first.

The relaxed one's head should fall back if she or he is truly relaxed. It may take several experiences with this exercise before children can trust one another.

Discuss how it feels.

Trust Jumps

Objective: To develop trust in one another.

Consideration: Ample space is required.

Directions: "One person should lie on the floor. Be still. Your partner will now jump over you.... Now make your body into another shape, and your partner will jump over you again.... Now begin to roll slowly, and partner, you see if you can still jump over your rolling partner. Take care of each other."

Contact

Objective: To isolate a point of contact and then always be aware of where that point of contact is.

Considerations: Ample space is required. This activity is appropriate for older children.

Directions: "Stand with your hands on each other's shoulders. Like this." Demonstrate with one couple. "Now, very carefully, don't move your feet but bring your heads together until they are

touching and you are leaning against each other's heads. Put
your hands down so that all that is touching is your heads. There
is just one contact point. Now I want you to always keep your
heads touching and nowhere else, but turn your bodies slowly so
that this contact point moves to another place on your head. Feel
which way your partner wants to go. Keep turning and keep
moving very slowly. Always keep the point of contact. Never lose
contact but let the point travel all around your head. Turn in the
other direction if you need to. You decide together how you turn
but always keep that point of contact. Stop. Be separate and shake
your bodies out. Shake all over. Beautiful. That was a very difficult
thing to do. You really had to work hard to always keep that point
of contact. Did you like the way it felt?"

Extensions: The point of contact may be any two parts of the
body; and they can be two different parts of the body, e.g., the
shoulder of one partner is pushing against the hip of the other
partner. The points of contact are changed by rolling along the
other person's body until you both come to a new place.

Note: A high degree of control is needed in this activity.

Activities for group participation: movement and body awareness

Shape Sculptures

Objectives: To acquire awareness of the possibilities of group
shape. To feel a connection with others.

Considerations: Can be done in a limited space. A drum is useful.
Divide group into two equal sections who will work together.

Directions: "I would like half of the class over here with me. The other half will move while I count from 1 to 10. When I reach 10, freeze in a shape. 1, 2, 3, 4, 5, 6, 7, 8, 9, 10. Freeze! Now this time, when I reach 10, freeze in a connected shape. You should be connected to someone else. 1, 2, 3, 4, 5, 6, 7, 8, 9, 10. Freeze! Now I would like the group that is watching—we will call you the Number Twos—to arrange yourself in shapes around the Number Ones. Now Number Ones melt down into the floor and come over to me. Number Twos stay frozen."

The shapes that are made can be very interesting and unexpected. Comment briefly on them but keep things moving by repeating the exercise several times. To keep things interesting, vary the number of times you count before one group arranges itself around the other.

Extensions: When the children freeze into shapes, have them freeze with a quality or a movement element in mind: twisted, at a high level, in a monstrous shape, etc.

Note: This activity sounds complicated, but if the directions are read carefully and each step is visualized, it will become clear.

The House

Objectives: To create a structure together. To work with the group to create a moving structure.

Considerations: Can be done in a limited space. Ten children at a time should work. The others can sit and watch.

Directions: "Everyone, down on the floor on your stomachs. Wiggle over until you are connected to another person. You should all be connected to one another now. I would like to see you very slowly rise to your feet still touching the same places on the people you are touching now. Very slowly. Everyone get up together. Everyone is all connected. Freeze! Now can you become a house for me?" Sit in the center of the children's structure. "Stay as connected as you can and make my house very small. Now make it very large with lots of windows. Now very small again and it will melt into the floor and everyone should roll to her or his own separate place."

Extensions: Children can be on the inside.
  Have the structure move.

Notes: Do not be too rigid about maintaining the original connections. Aim for connections other than hand-to-hand connections so that the shape is more interesting.

The Machine

Objectives: To become a part of a group which creates a total image. To develop repetitions of sound and movement. To understand rhythms.

Considerations: Can be done in a limited space as a total class activity. This activity is appropriate for older children.

Directions: "Everyone come over here and sit down next to me. George, show me how you think a machine looks. Can you make a noise that goes with what you are doing? A very machinelike noise. Esther. You are another part of that machine out there. What part are you? What noise do you make as you work? Susan, now it's your turn. You know, your part of this machine can move more slowly or more quickly than the other parts of the machine."

  Add children until a total machine is created. Encourage them to be at different levels, to make different kinds of sounds (some with just air and some voiced), to make very small movements or very large movements, and to make movements with parts of the body besides just the arms and hands. It can dissolve into a heap or else freeze and then parts can be removed one by one.

Extensions: See if the machine can move through space. If it can, make it go faster, slower, or in paths.

Activities for group participation: strength and groundedness

Tunnels and Bridges

Objectives: To create ways of moving over and under others. To feel strength in unity with others.

Considerations: Can be done in a limited space. To be done with groups of three or more. Begin by dividing the group into threes and then combining groups or coming back and repeating the activity another time with larger groups.

Directions: "Come sit by me. Now, I would like Talya to go over and make a shape that is very firm and strong. One that you can hold for a while. Good. Now, Maria, you walk over and make a shape in front of Talya that is attached to hers that is also very firm and strong. OK. Eli, now it's your turn. Make a shape in front of Maria that is connected to her that is very firm and strong. Oh, your shape is supported by her shape. That will be very interesting. Make sure you can hold that shape for a while."

Continue in this way until all of the children are in a line of strong shapes.

"Now Talya is at the end of the line, and she is going to find a place to start where she is going to crawl over you and wriggle through you and slither under you until she comes out in front of Melina and then Talya will become a strong shape attached in front of Melina."

Children should be encouraged to help one another over and under without breaking the formation too drastically. When the first child assumes her or his shape, make sure there is plenty of room left for the rest of the line to take shape.

Extension: Change the number of children in a group.

Notes: The younger the children, the smaller the groups should be. The younger children will need more supervision and assistance. Watch carefully and be ready to assist physically when necessary.

Activities for group participation: trust and sensitivity

Rock-A-Bye Baby

Objectives: To care for someone. To enjoy participation in a group that is joined together in an effort. To feel a rhythmic movement. To allow oneself to be cared for.

Considerations: Can be done in a limited space. The group sizes are determined by the size of the children. How many children's backs side by side do you need to make a bed? Five-year-olds require about five backs and eight-year-olds require about seven backs. This works well with younger children.

Directions: "We can rock someone on our backs. Go on to your hands and knees as though you are going to crawl. Put yourselves side by side, so your backs make a bed for Julie. Now, Julie, you very gently lie down on your bed."

Sing "Rock-A-Bye Baby" and when the bough breaks and the cradle falls, everyone collapse together. Make sure everyone has a chance to lie on the bed.

Extensions: Make up a song as you sway back and forth or make a rhythmic sound. At the end, gently ease the child down so that she or he can roll onto the floor.

The Cradle

Objectives: To care for one another. To enjoy the feeling of being cared for. To feel rhythmic movement.

Considerations: Can be done in a limited space with groups of three to six children.

Directions: "Let's figure out how we can make a cradle for someone if we sit together. Ezra, you can be the first baby. Now let's figure out how to make a cradle for Ezra." Once the cradle is made and the child is being rocked, you can sing a lullaby.

Notes: While the child is being rocked, talk about how nice it is for everyone to be a baby again for a while and about how nice it is to take care of people. Discourage excessive silliness. This activity is more threatening than *Rock-A-Bye Baby* because there is easier eye contact between the participants. Be sure everyone has a chance to be the baby. Playing both roles is of importance.

Lifting Others

Objectives: To care for others. To understand the weight of others and how your strength combined with others can be used.

Considerations: Can be done in a limited space with groups of four to eight children.

Directions: "Let's figure out a way to gently lift a person. Who would like to be lifted? OK. Pepe you can be the first person lifted.

I would like you to lie down on the floor. I would like the rest of us to kneel all around him like this." Put yourself at the head of the child. Kneel, sitting back on your heels. Make certain that most of the children are by the torso rather than the legs. "First I would like you to very gently rest your hands on Pepe's body." Put your hands on his chest with your palms down. "We have a job to take care of Pepe when we lift him. Your gentle hands resting on him now tell him that you are going to care for him when you lift him. Now very slowly slide your hands under Pepe's body. And now when I reach 3 we will all lift and stand up together. 1, 2, 3." Everyone lifts and stands up. "We aren't going to go anywhere. Beautiful. Now when I reach 3 let's very gently put him down. This is really the hardest part. You must be very careful and gentle. 1, 2, 3."

Extensions: Sway the lifted person back and forth.
    Carry the person to a specified point.
    Allow the children to figure out how to lift you.

Notes: Everyone should have a chance to be the lifted one.
    At some point, discuss where people are the heaviest and what happens if no one is lifting at the torso.

Rolling Over

Objectives: To be part of a group that is providing a special experience for another. To understand weight both as a supporter and as the supported one.

Considerations: Can be done in a limited space with groups of 6 to 12 children.

Directions: "I would like you to lie down side by side. The person at the end will figure out how to gently roll over the others until she or he is lying at the other end. Then the next one will begin. Take care of each other."

Notes: Knees, elbows, and heads cannot take much weight. Also, knees and elbows can really dig into the supporters' backs. Point this out to children as they are working.

Heavier children may be hesitant. Deal with this by reassuring them that the people on the bottom are strong. Different people are different weights. The more relaxed the rolling person can be, the more evenly distributed the weight will be. Keeping the children moving means no one supports the weight for very long. Everyone should be both on the bottom and on the top. Encourage discussion.

Crawling Over

Objectives: To be a part of a group that is providing a special experience for another. To understand weight and its distribution, both as a supporter and as the supported one.

Considerations: Can be done in a limited space with groups of 6 to 12 children.

Directions: "I would like everyone to get in a crawling position. Now line up side by side. The person on the end is going to crawl over your backs. It is important that you be very firm and grounded so that you offer a good support for the person who is crawling. The person who is crawling must be very careful to put hands and knees where they can be supported best."

Notes: Because the weight is concentrated in the hands and the knees, children must place those body parts carefully where that pressure can best be taken (at the hips and shoulders of the bottom supporters). See the notes for *Rolling Over* (p. 144).

Fantasy work

Fantasy work can provide an opportunity for children to graphically explore some of the fantasies and concerns of childhood. Many children are concerned with robbers, disasters, death, monsters, being lost or deserted, breaking bones, jail, and so on. By listening to children carefully and reading the stories they write, you can pick up other topics with which to work. These fantasies can also be an opportunity to deal with topics which the teacher thinks are important. For example, what do you do if there is a fire in your house, how does it feel to be left out by others, what do you do if you are lost, how does it feel to be made fun of, how does it feel to be angry, and what can you do to feel better.

Here are two ways of acting out fantasies.

Method 1: teacher participation

This method is more suitable for working with small groups of children. Begin a story and ask questions of the children as you proceed. Allow the answers to alter the direction the fantasy takes. Let everyone do the actions together. Sometimes you will find that someone will have to play a principal role or that a group of people may play a particular function. The fantasies can be repeated again and again with different people playing different roles.

Example: "Look what happened! Loren has hurt himself. What happened?" At this point Loren will have made himself look suitably stricken on the floor. "He broke his leg? Oh, what are we going to do now? Call the doctor? OK, who would like to stay here and take care of Loren while we go over here and phone the doctor?" Half the group runs over and pantomimes telephoning the doctor. The other half takes care of Loren. "We have to take him to the hospital. Let's pick him up carefully and take him over. Poor Loren, is he going to be OK? Take good care of him. It must hurt, poor leg. If we hold his hand, will he feel better? Here comes the doctor. What is she going to do? Make the bone so it is straight. OK, let's straighten the bone." Everyone straightens imaginary bones. "Now what? We put a cast on the leg. OK, let's put the cast on. How does it feel to have a cast on your leg? It's heavy? And you can't bend your leg any more either, can you?

Let's all have casts on our legs. I can't go very fast. This isn't very much fun. How long do I have to wear this? Let's take off the casts now and have our legs be all better. When we first take off the cast we are kind of slow at moving our leg, aren't we? It has to get used to moving and carrying us again. But now it's feeling better. Now I can run and jump and skip just like before. Look what I can do now that my leg is well!"

There are no rules. As often as not the patient dies from the broken leg and is buried under the ground and everyone ends up feeling sad unless somehow it turns out that the person can be resurrected.

Method 2: teacher direction

Begin a story and let each child act out the fantasy in her or his own way in her or his own space. The children can be moved from a point of stillness and groundedness to a place of high activity and back to stillness again.

As the fantasy proceeds, watch the children carefully to see what individual children are doing. Alter what is happening in the fantasy to reflect what is happening with the children. If they are tadpoles swimming in the water and they are really enjoying this moment, extend the moment by having them dive for a morsel of food or have them dart away from a big fish which is coming their way.

This method of fantasy-making can be used for developing themes such as: a seed growing into a tree, a rock lying at the bottom of a volcano, an egg which hatches into a bird, an egg which becomes a larva which becomes a pupa which becomes a moth, a person lying in a bed who gets up and slays a dragon.

Example: "Everyone find your own space on the floor and lie down. You are now in your own bed at home. The lights are out and it is very dark. You want to go to sleep, but you just can't. You turn over and try to be comfortable, and you turn over again, and you just can't get to sleep. So you decide to get up and you go over and open the door and instead of the hallway, there is a sandy beach outside your bedroom door! The sun is bright and warm, and you feel like just stretching out and running in that sand.

Let's run and feel that sand under our feet. You're the only person on this beach and it feels just glorious to run and run under that warm, warm sun. Run and run and run. Finally you're kind of tired so you flop down on the sand and you feel it under your feet and legs so you kind of dig down with your toes and kick the sand up. You kick the sand way up in the air. Now kick your legs way up in the air. This is terrific! You can just roll and roll in this sand, so you roll and roll and you roll into the ocean and you start swimming. You can swim just like a fish. You don't even need to come up for air. The water is all smooth around you and takes care of you. You could swim forever. Let's stand up and swim. You move so smoothly through the water. You're just like a fish. Let's dive down and swim under that rock. There's a strange plant there. We've gotten all tangled up. It's all wrapped around you, you can't move. Be very calm. Look and feel where you are caught. Now slowly break it away. Break it off of you. You can do it. Push it away. You're sure glad to get rid of that. You start swimming again. Dive back down to the floor and start rolling in the water. Roll and roll until you're back in your own bed. Sound asleep. You're sound asleep again in your own bed. Just relax there. Rest."

Both methods of fantasy-making are useful. The choice should depend on the position the teacher wants to take in relationship to the children. If you want to maintain a firm control over the group, then choose the teacher-direction method. If you want a more familiar, less controlled experience then choose the teacher-participation method.

With each approach, decide beforehand on a theme so that a fantasy can be started quickly when appropriate.

Activities for ending a session

Relaxation and touching

Speak in a low, unhurried voice. "I want you to melt down to the floor. Now roll your body to your own space. A place where you can be by yourself and feel the ground under you. Feel the ground and feel your body against it. The ground is holding you up, taking care of you. Now breathe in through your nose and let the breath go to the center of you—somewhere near your belly button—and let the breath out through your mouth. Feel your breath go in and out. I am going to come around now, and I am going to touch your shoulders. I'll know when you are ready for me to come to you by your stillness. Listen to the sounds that come into the room. Let the sounds just flow over you. No one can disturb you. You are safe in your own place right now."

At this point, go around and touch the part of the body you told the children you would touch. Massage the flesh around that part of the body with a firm touch or simply apply a firm, still pressure. Talk about what that body part does. This is an appropriate time to talk to each child quietly about some aspect of her or his work you noticed that day. It is a time to directly communicate to each child in a tactile and/or verbal way.

Many children look forward to this part of the class. It is important that the children feel safe during this activity. No one should be permitted to disturb the children physically or verbally. Once you have touched the children, they are free to get up and to quietly walk over and put on their shoes or else to lie there quietly or even to talk quietly to a friend. You must make sure that the children you come to last are not disturbed before you have a chance to massage them.

Tightening and relaxing body parts

"Now I want you to clench your fists and make them tight, tight, tight, while I count to 5. 1, 2, 3, 4, 5. Now let your fists relax.

Just let them be. They should feel all tingly and good. Now make your shoulders and arms and hands all tight, like you did your fists, while I count to 5."

Continue the tightening and loosening of other parts of the body: head and face, screwing them all up; whole upper torso; toes and feet, like a fist; feet and legs; whole body. Lead up to a period of quiet time at the end where the children just feel their bodies relaxed upon the ground. At this time you can go around and briefly massage each child.

Part IV: Activities for One Child and One Adult Working Together

Chapter 6: Movement sessions for one child and one adult

These activities can be done at the park, during lunchtime or recess, or as a special activity at the end of class. They are best done when you want to play physically with the children or when you want to relate to a particular child in a physical way. Some of these activities will be familiar because they are often the ways adults, such as parents, relate to children physically. They are included because they are ways to have fun together, ways for a child to learn more about her or his abilities safely, and ways to develop trust in one another.

Perhaps you can remember playing wonderful, intimate games like "This Little Piggy Went to Market" in your childhood. Try to remember your own childhood games and pass them on to continue your own rich cultural tradition. Almost all of the activities for partners (pp. 125 – 137) can be done by an adult with a child. Many of the activities for three- and four-year-olds can be modified so that they are appropriate for one child and one adult working together.

Movement and body awareness

1. You and the child stand facing each other and hold hands. When the child jumps, you can apply pressure at the right moment to the child's hands and arms so you can lift the child to a higher jump.

Activities for one child and one adult such as this are fun, help children learn more about their abilities safely, and are ways to develop trust in one another.

2. You and the child stand facing each other and hold hands. The shoeless child begins to walk up your body until she or he is upside down. At this point the child can balance in this position or else the child can continue the circular movement, ending up back on the floor facing you.

3. You sit on the ground. The child stands behind your shoulder facing the same direction you are facing. The child leans over your shoulder so that you can receive the upper part of the child's body with your hands, and you can then help the child's head tuck into a somersault between your legs. The child's head needs to be tucked through her or his arms so that the spine has a good curve. The adult can reverse the operation so that the child is doing a backward roll up over the adult's shoulder. The child can also do somersaults over your knee. It is most important in somersaults that children really tuck their heads so that their spines have a nice curve.

4. Stand and hold a child in your arms with her or his legs around your waist. Let the top half of the child's body fall back and gently swing the child. The child can put her or his hands on the ground and do a handstand turn-over to the ground.

5. Stand with your legs placed apart firmly. The child lies on her or his back. You lift the child firmly by the heels until the child

is standing on her or his hands. The child can then walk on the hands through your legs until the body is roughly parallel with the ground. You need a strong back and small children for this since you must lift their full weight.

6. Imitate a child's movement. Be very sensitive when doing this. There must be no hint of ridicule—only pleasure in trying someone else's way of moving.

Strength and groundedness

1. Make a trap with your body so that the child must push against you with all her or his strength to get out. Be very sensitive to when the child should be able to succeed. The child should feel the adult strength but eventually you should yield to the child.

2. Be like an adult ape on all fours with the child clinging underneath you. Now move around.

3. Arrange your body so that you are very solid, perhaps standing with hands on slightly bent knees. The shoeless child can climb around and about you as though you are a climbing apparatus. The child is very safe however because you can shift weight to help the child and are right there to break the fall.

The child's feeling of success and personal strength when she makes her escape is our goal.

4. Wrestling. Just plain wrestling. Wrestle with just one child at a time. Be very serious. Allow the child to really feel a personal strength. This is an excellent way for a female teacher to let the female children know that wrestling is all right for girls to do too.

5. A child curls up very tightly. You tug at parts of the child, testing the child's strength. Make certain the child has a tucked head. If you pick up the child, can the child maintain that curled-up position?

6. The child lies flat on the ground, belly down, and the adult tries to pry the child up. You can feel whether the child is centering strength where you are pulling. Verbally encourage the child to put her or his strength where you are pulling. The child should always manage to remain flat.

7. Stand facing a child. Push with your hands against the child's hands, balancing your strength and weight with the child's. If the child is small, it may be necessary for you to kneel.

Trust and sensitivity

1. Swing a child around holding her or him under the arms or around the waist. The child's body may be extended or curled up.

2. Make a house with your body for a child to curl up into. Have this house be a safe, nurturing place.

3. Cradle a child and sing a lullaby. Let the child pretend to be a baby.

4. Lie down. Hold a child in your arms and roll across the ground with the child.

5. Lie down on your back and balance children in a variety of ways on your hands and feet. Children can stand on your hands with your upstretched legs and feet to hang onto for balance for a different kind of balancing experience. All of you will feel like you are in the circus when the child can stand with no support on your hands! You need strong arms if you try to extend your arms so the child is standing high.

6. The child stands facing you and falls onto your waiting hands. The child's body should be somewhat rigid so the child

does not collapse in the middle. The adult can move farther and farther away, involving more and more trust. The child can also fall backward. If the child cannot relax enough to fall, put one hand on the front of the child's chest and one hand on the back of the chest so that the body feels supported to the child. Gradually bring the child's weight onto the front chest hand.

7. Cover your eyes so you cannot see and have the child guide you around the room.

8. Roll on the ground and have the child jump over you.

9. Be limp on the ground. Ask the child (or children) to figure out how to carry you, drag you, push you, roll you, or arrange your body in various shapes. Let the child know what feels OK and what does not. Do not tell the child what to do.

10. The child lies flat on the ground on her or his back. You straddle the body facing the head and take hold of the child's wrists. Lift the upper torso so that you can sway the torso from side to side. Gently lower the child back to the floor. If the child is very relaxed the head will fall back loosely. Sometimes you need to ask the child to let her or his head fall back. Let the child do this same thing to you. It feels wonderful.

Bibliography

Ayres, A. J. *Sensory Integration and Learning Disorders.* Los Angeles: Western Psychological Services, 1972–73.

Ayres, A. J. *Sensory Integration and the Child.* Los Angeles: Western Psychological Services, 1979. This book tells what sensory integration is all about.

Baker, K. R. *Let's Play Outdoors.* Rev. ed. Washington, D.C.: National Association for the Education of Young Children, 1966. A practical, thoughtful group of suggestions for the inexpensive development of outdoor spaces.

Barlin, A. L. *Teaching Your Wings to Fly: The Nonspecialist's Guide to Movement Activities for Young Children.* Santa Monica, Calif.: Goodyear, 1979. A good book on teaching dance to children. Most activities are designed for children older than six years.

Bayless, K. M., and Ramsey, M. E. *Music: A Way of Life for the Young Child.* 2nd ed. St. Louis: Mosby, 1982. A comprehensive, useful book.

Bicanich, D. D., and Manke, C. W. *Sensori-Motor Activity Guide for Preschoolers from Birth to Age Five.* West St. Paul, Minn.: Bicanich & Manke, 1978. A well-done, easy-to-use book with many movement suggestions. Must be ordered directly: 1340 Seminole Ave., West St. Paul, MN 55118.

Carr, R. *Be a Frog, a Bird, or a Tree: Creative Yoga Exercises for Children.* Garden City, N.Y.: Doubleday, 1973. Useful for small group movement activities in the classroom.

Courlander, H. *Negro Songs from Alabama.* Published in collaboration with the Wenner-Gren Foundation for Anthropological Research, New York, N.Y. 1960.

Ellison, G. *Play Structures: Questions to Discuss, Designs to Consider, Directions for Construction.* Pasadena, Calif.: Pacific Oaks College and Children's School, 1974.

Engstrom, G., ed. *The Significance of the Young Child's Motor Development.* Washington, D.C.: National Association for the Education of Young Children, 1971. A beautiful explanation of the reasons why we teach movement to young children.

Fluegelman, A., ed. *The New Games Book.* New York: Doubleday, 1976.

Glazer, T. *Eye Winker, Tom Tinker, Chin Chopper: Fifty Musical Fingerplays.* Garden City, N.Y.: Doubleday, 1973. Useful material for bringing groups of preschoolers together.

Glazer, T. *Do Your Ears Hang Low?: 50 More Musical Fingerplays.* Garden City, N.Y.: Doubleday, 1980.

Hendricks, G., and Wills, R. *The Centering Book: Awareness Activities for Children, Parents, and Teachers.* Englewood Cliffs, N.J.: Prentice-Hall, 1975. Good techniques for relaxations.

Hill, D. M. *Mud, Sand, and Water*. Washington, D.C.: National Association for the Education of Young Children, 1977. Curriculum ideas that emphasize the importance of mud, sand, and water as messy—but essential—tools for children's healthy development.

Jones, B., and Hawes, B. L. *Step It Down: Games, Plays, Songs, and Stories from the Afro-American Heritage*. New York: Harper & Row, 1972. In addition to good material, there is a rich child philosophy expressed.

Jones, E. *Dimensions of Teaching-Learning Environments: Handbook for Teachers*. Pasadena, Calif.: Pacific Oaks College, 1973. This book has important information on designing environments for young children, including large motor areas and classroom areas.

Joyce, M. *First Steps in Teaching Creative Dance: A Handbook for Teachers of Children, Kindergarten through Sixth Grade*. Palo Alto, Calif.: Mayfield Publishing Co., 1973. An excellent book.

Kamii, C., and DeVries, R. *Group Games in Early Education: Implications of Piaget's Theory*. Washington, D.C.: National Association for the Education of Young Children, 1980.

Kantner, R. M.; Clark, D. L.; Allen, L. C.; and Chase, M. F. "Effects of Vestibular Stimulation on Nystagmus Response and Motor Performance in the Developmentally Delayed Infant." *Physical Therapy* 56 (1976): 414 – 421.

Kogan, S. *Step By Step: A Complete Movement Education Curriculum from Preschool to 6th Grade*. Byron, Calif.: Front Row Experience, 1982. An excellent, practical book, especially for elementary teachers.

Laban, R. *Modern Educational Dance*. London: Macdonald & Evans, Ltd., 1948. British Infant Schools have based their teaching of movement upon this wonderful book.

Landeck, B. ed. *Songs to Grow On: A Collection of American Folk Songs for Children*. New York: Edward B. Marks Music Corporation and William Sloane Associates, Inc., 1950. Folk songs and play party games with suggested movement activities.

Landeck, B., and Crook, E., eds. *Wake Up and Sing!: Folk Songs from America's Grassroots*. New York: Edward B. Marks Music Corporation and William Morrow, 1969. This collection includes many of Woody Guthrie's songs that are especially appropriate for the very young.

McDonald, D. T. *Music in Our Lives: The Early Years*. Washington, D.C.: National Association for the Education of Young Children, 1977. Meaningful and enjoyable musical experiences for children from infancy through age six.

May, B. *T.S.K.H. (Tickle Snug Kiss Hug)*. New York: The Paulist Press, 1977. There is a great deal of useful material in this book for anyone teaching movement to children.

Milberg, A. *Street Games*. New York: McGraw-Hill, 1976. A reminder of all the good material from our own childhoods.

Mogar, N. Personal communication, 1980.

Moore, R. C. *Childhood's Domain: Play and Place in Child Development.* London: Croomhelm, 1983. Moore is an advocate of naturalistic play environments for children.

Olatunji, M. *Drums of Passion and More Drums of Passion.* Columbia Record #CG33654. Columbia Records, 51 W. 52 St., New York, NY 10019.

Orlick, T. *The Cooperative Sports & Games Book: Challenge Without Competition.* New York: Pantheon, 1978. Good material for three- to seven-year-olds.

Orlick, T. *The Second Cooperative Sports & Games Book.* New York: Pantheon, 1982. A very thoughtful book with ideas from all over the world. Again, good material for three- to seven-year-olds.

Ring Games Alabama. Folkways Record #7004. Folkways Records, 43 W. 61 St., New York, NY 10023.

Seeger, R. C., ed. *American Folk Songs for Children.* Garden City, N.Y.: Doubleday, 1948. A wonderful collection with good information on using the material.

Skeen, P.; Garner, A. P.; and Cartwright, S. *Woodworking for Young Children.* Washington, D.C.: National Association for the Education of Young Children, 1983.

Slobodkina, E. *Caps for Sale.* Reading, Mass.: Addison-Wesley, 1940.

Spencer, R. A. *Early Childhood Music Kit.* New York: Trillium Press, 1980.

Stecher, M. B.; McElheny, H.; and Greenwood, M. *Joy and Learning Through Music and Movement Improvisations.* New York: Macmillan, 1972. An excellent book on developing improvisational musical activities with children.

Walsh, R. N., and Greenough, W. T., eds. *Environmental Therapy for Brain Disorder.* New York: Plenum, 1976. Proceedings of the 1975 Winter Conference on Brain Research held in Steamboat Springs, Colorado, January 1975.

Westland, C., and Knight, J. *Playing, Living, Learning: A Worldwide Perspective on Children's Opportunities to Play.* State College, Pa.: Venture, 1982. A book that explores some exciting ideas for the development of outdoor spaces.

Winn, M. *What Shall We Do and Allee Galloo!* New York: Harper & Row, 1970.

Information about NAEYC

NAEYC is . . .

. . . a membership organization of people committed to fostering the growth and development of children from birth through age eight. Membership is open to all who share a desire to serve and act on behalf of the needs and rights of young children.

NAEYC provides . . .

. . . educational services and resources to adults who work with and for children, including

- **Young Children,** *the* Journal for early childhood educators.
- **Books, posters, and brochures** to expand our knowledge and commitment to young children. Topics include infants, curriculum, research, discipline, teacher education, and parent involvement.
- An **Annual Conference** that brings people from all over the world to share their expertise and advocate on behalf of children and families.
- **Week of the Young Child** celebrations sponsored by NAEYC Affiliate Groups across the country to call public attention to the needs and rights of children and families.
- **Insurance plans** for individuals and programs.
- **Public policy information** for informed advocacy efforts at all levels of government.
- The **National Academy of Early Childhood Programs,** a voluntary accreditation system for high quality programs for young children.

For **free** information about membership, publications, or other NAEYC services . . .

. . . call NAEYC toll free at 800-424-2460 or 202-232-8777 or write to **NAEYC, 1834 Connecticut Avenue, N.W., Washington, DC 20009.**